CHRISTIANITY EXPLORED

Authentic

First published in 2001 by Paternoster Lifestyle
Second edition published in 2003 by Authentic Lifestyle
Reprinted 2003

10 09 08 07 06 05 04   9 8 7 6 5 4 3

Reprinted 2004 by Authentic Media
9 Holdom Avenue, Bletchley, Milton Keynes, MK1 1QR
and Box 1047, Waynesboro, GA 30830-2047, USA
www.authenticmedia.co.uk

British Library Cataloguing in Publication Data
A catalogue record for this book is available from the British Library

ISBN 1-85078-523-6

Designed by Diane Bainbridge
Print Management by Adare Carwin

CHRISTIANITY E✞PLORED

STUDY GUIDE

LEADER'S EDITION

SECTION 1 - TRAINING NOTES

SECTION 2 - STUDY GUIDE

Welcome to **Christianity Explored**.

During the ten-week course, as Mark's Gospel is read and taught, you will be helping participants to explore three questions that cut right to the heart of Christianity: Who was Jesus? Why did he come? What does Jesus demand of those who want to follow him?

In other words, it's all about Jesus' identity, mission and call.

The first six weeks focus on Christ's identity and mission. In particular, course participants explore the problem of sin and the wonder of forgiveness.

There is then a weekend or day away when participants can find out about the church, the Holy Spirit, prayer and the Bible.

The objective in the final weeks is to emphasize Christ's call in Mark 8:34 – "If anyone would come after me, he must deny himself and take up his cross and follow me."

This book is divided into two sections: the first will train you to use the course, and the second will be your guide each week as you actually run the course.

CHRISTIANITY E✝PLORED

SECTION 1
TRAINING NOTES

This section will prepare you to lead participants
through the course. You should cover the sessions on
a training day with your course leader.

WHY EVANGELIZE?

➢ Write down your answer to this question:

> **What images come to mind when you hear the word "evangelist"?**
>
> *Someone who is keen to go out & tell the good news of Jesus Christ. Burnstop & tell & share the news. Anxious for all to hear the news.*

Everyone has an image of what an "evangelist" is like. Some people think of a Bible-bashing, street-preaching fanatic. Others think of a money-grubbing, brainwashing TV personality.

Unfortunately, these popular images of the evangelist have sometimes kept us from obeying the Bible's clear command to evangelize (see, for example, Matthew 28:18–20; Luke 24:47; Acts 1:8; 1 Corinthians 9:16; 2 Corinthians 5:11; 2 Timothy 4:1–5).

➢ Now write down your answers to these questions:

> **Which Christian person most strongly influenced your decision to follow Christ?**
>
> *Grandmother first of all. George Bungles*

> **What words describe this person and his or her attitude toward you?**
>
> *I saw how real my grandmother's faith was to her. She spoke of it all the time. George Bungles was so sure of his faith.*

There is probably a big difference between the stereotypical image of an evangelist and the actual person who "evangelized" you. Most of us put our trust in Christ because of Christians who treated us in a patient, caring, sincere way. That means we all have what it takes to be an evangelist.

And we will do the work of an evangelist when we recognize that:

1. everyone has a role in evangelism

2. hell and heaven are real

3. people matter to God

1. EVERYONE HAS A ROLE IN EVANGELISM

➤ *Read 2 Corinthians 5:18–20.*

All of us are "Christ's ambassadors, as though God were making his appeal through us." And the appeal we make to others is straightforward: "Be reconciled to God."

But there are different ways to communicate this message, as the New Testament demonstrates. You will find that you are more comfortable with some than others:[1]

Confrontational
confident, bold, direct, skips small talk, gets right to the point, has strong convictions and opinions
see for example Peter in Acts 2:14–40

Intellectual
analytical, logical, inquisitive, likes to debate ideas, more concerned with what people think than with what they feel
see for example Paul in Acts 17:16–31

Testimonial
good story teller, passionate about the account of how God rescued them, sees links between their own experience and others
see for example the blind man in John 9:1–33

---

[1] Adapted from *Becoming a Contagious Christian: Participant's Guide* by Mark Mittelberg, Lee Strobel and Bill Hybels © Willow Creek Association. Used by permission. Part of a training course that includes a questionnaire to help you further identify your evangelism style and gives you practical steps for developing that style.

CHRISTIANITY
E✝PLORED

Interpersonal

conversational, compassionate, sensitive, friendship-oriented, focuses on people and their needs

see for example Levi in Luke 5:27–29

Invitational

hospitable, persuasive, enjoys meeting new people, committed to things he or she believes in, asks people to come and hear the good news

see for example the woman at the well in John 4:4–30

Serving

patient, sees other people's needs and finds joy in meeting them, expresses love in actions more than words, sees the value in performing menial tasks

see for example Dorcas in Acts 9:36

The Bible makes it clear that there are many, many different ways in which we can evangelize. Each one of us has our own skills, temperaments and experiences that make us uniquely able to tell others about God.

2. HELL AND HEAVEN ARE REAL

We will also be motivated to evangelize when we take Jesus' words about hell and heaven seriously.

➤ *Read Luke 16:19–31.*

Verses 23 and 24 describe hell as a place of suffering. Jesus tells us that the rich man was: "In hell, where he was in torment." He was in a physical place where he was in "agony." Verse 26 adds that hell is a place of separation from God. And notice that the rich man wants to warn his brothers about hell. Tragically, he has become a keen evangelist now that it is too late.

If people go through life accepting God's gifts while ignoring the giver, as the rich man has done in verse 25, then hell – according to Jesus – is where they are headed. Jesus makes it very clear that our sin will lead us to hell: "If your hand causes you to sin, cut it off. It is better for you to enter life maimed than with two hands to go into hell, where the fire never goes out" (Mark 9:43).

We learn from verse 22 of the parable that heaven is a physical place too: "The beggar died and the angels carried him to Abraham's side." But, unlike hell, heaven is a place of comfort (v. 25), a place that God has prepared for all those who love him. There will be no more "death or mourning or crying or pain" (Revelation 21:4). There will be no more separation; God will live with us (Revelation 21:3). In other words, it will be a place free from sin and its effects.

But it is dishonest to welcome what Jesus says about heaven without also accepting what he says about hell.

The reality of hell – where people will be eternally separated from God and from us – should motivate us all to evangelize.

3. PEOPLE MATTER TO GOD

You will never set eyes upon someone who does not matter to God. And as long as that is true, we must continue to do the work of evangelists.

➤ Read Luke 15:1–32.

In each of these three parables, something that is of great value to someone goes missing – a sheep, a coin, a son. In each case, the lost item represents the lost "sinner."

Each parable illustrates how much the lost matter to the Father. The shepherd goes after the sheep until he finds it (v. 4); the woman sweeps the house and searches carefully until she finds the coin (v. 8); the father's eyes scan the horizon for his son (v. 20). In fact, we matter so much to God that he sent his Son to search for us and pay the ultimate price on our behalf.

Jesus tells us that finding what was lost merits great celebration. Indeed, verses 7 and 10 show us that there was rejoicing in heaven on the day we were reunited with God.

You will never set eyes upon someone who does not matter to God, who does not warrant an all-out search, and for whom the whole of heaven would not rejoice if he or she were to bow down and confess Christ as Lord.

CHRISTIANITY
EXPLORED

GOD'S PART IN EVANGELISM — AND OURS

We need to distinguish between God's part in evangelism and our part. It's going to be incredibly frustrating if we try to do God's part – because only the creator of the universe is able to do that.

➤ *Read 2 Corinthians 4:1–6.*

➤ *Answer the following questions from the verses you've just read:*

What is God's part in evangelism?

Opening our eyes to someer

Why can't people see the truth of the gospel?

Their eyes are not open

What is our part in evangelism?

We must be in the firing line tell it & leave god to convert. Tell it honestly relying on god,

How should we do our part in evangelism?

Tell it prayerfully. not promoting ourselves, Pray for a miracle. Straight genuine Sincere. depend on Holy Spirit

---

According to these verses, what is God's part in evangelism? God makes "his light shine in our hearts to give us the light of the knowledge of the glory of God in the face of Christ" (v. 6).

In other words, God enables us to recognize that Jesus is God. God makes it possible – by his Holy Spirit – for a person to see who Jesus is. When Paul is on the Damascus Road, he asks, "Who are you Lord?" and is told, "I am Jesus" (Acts 9:5). That is the moment of his conversion – when he recognizes for the first time who Jesus actually is.

The beginning of verse 6 reminds us that God said, "Let light shine out of darkness." That is a reference to the miracle of creation in Genesis 1:3. This same God who brought light into the world at creation now shines light into the hearts of human beings, enabling them to see that Jesus is God. In other words, for people to recognize that Jesus is God, God must perform a miracle.

People do not become Christians just because we share the gospel with them. God must shine his light in people's hearts so that they recognize and respond to the truth of the gospel.

According to 2 Corinthians 4:1–6, why can't people see the truth of the gospel? "The god of this age has blinded the minds of unbelievers" (v. 4).

Here, Paul reminds us that we are in the middle of a supernatural battlefield. The reason so many reject the gospel is that the devil is at work preventing people from recognizing who Jesus is.

The devil blinds people by making them chase after the things of this world, which are passing away, and cannot save them. Their concerns are totally confined to the here and now: the career, the family, the mortgage, the relationship. They are blind to anything beyond that.

As a result, they can only see Jesus in the here and now, perhaps as a great moral teacher; his eternal significance is completely obscured. And, according to verse 4, Satan is determined to prevent people from seeing "the light of the gospel of the glory of Christ, who is the image of God." Satan does not want people to recognize who Jesus is.

According to 2 Corinthians 4:1–6, what is our part in evangelism? "we... preach... Jesus Christ as Lord" (v. 5).

Our part is to tell people the gospel and leave the Spirit of God to convict them of its truth. The word "preach" can evoke negative images, but it derives from a word simply meaning "herald," someone who relates important announcements from the king to his kingdom.

Verse 5 also tells us the attitude we should adopt as we preach. We are to be like "servants for Jesus' sake." The word translated "servants" literally means "slaves" in Greek. Paul was determined to present Christ to others without any hint of self-promotion.

We must remember that the only difference between ourselves and an unbeliever is that God, in his mercy, has opened our blind eyes and illuminated our hearts by his Holy Spirit. We should be forever grateful, and so seek to promote Christ, not ourselves.

We must keep preaching Christ as Lord and, remembering that only a miracle from God can open blind eyes, we must keep praying that God will shine his light in the hearts of unbelievers.

According to 2 Corinthians 4:1–6, how should we do our part in evangelism? "We do not use deception, nor do we distort the word of God... by setting forth the truth plainly we commend ourselves to every man's conscience in the sight of God... For we do not preach ourselves, but Jesus Christ as Lord" (vv. 2, 5).

When we tell people about Christ, we should demonstrate the following qualities:

Integrity – "we do not use deception"
We are straight with people; we are genuine and sincere.

Fidelity – we do not "distort the word of God"
We have to tell people the tough bits. If – for example – we don't tell them about sin, about hell, and about the necessity of repentance, then we are distorting God's word. Preaching these hard truths means trusting in the work of the Holy Spirit to draw people to Christ, however "difficult" the message.

Intelligibility – we set forth "the truth plainly"

We should always ask ourselves the question, "Was that clear? Were people able to understand?"

Humility – "we do not preach ourselves, but Jesus Christ as Lord"

We must draw people to Jesus, not to ourselves.

As we use *Christianity Explored* to preach the gospel, we must remember that it is up to God whether somebody becomes a Christian or not. Only he can open blind eyes, so we must trust him for the results. God will do his part, and we must do ours.

CHRISTIANITY
EXPLORED

BEING A CHRISTIANITY EXPLORED LEADER

So, what will it be like to do our part in **Christianity Explored**?

➤ *Read 2 Timothy, chapters 1–2.*

With the joy that comes from seeing the lost rescued, we also see the sobering reality of the task ahead. In 2 Timothy 1:8, Paul beseeches Timothy to join him in "suffering" for the gospel. He wrote this around AD 67, chained and shackled in a Roman prison and aware that he was going to die soon. Many followers of Christ had deserted Paul (2 Timothy 1:15), so his appeal to Timothy is not only to join him in suffering for the gospel, but also to guard it, protect it and pass it on.

2 Timothy 2:1–4 is a good model for us as we lead participants through **Christianity Explored**. These verses describe the dedicated soldier for whom hardship, risk and suffering are a matter of course. Tertullian describes a soldier's life like this: "No soldier goes to war equipped with luxuries, nor does he go forth to the battle-line from his bed-chamber, but from light and narrow tents wherein every hardship and roughness and uncomfortableness is to be found."[2]

Being a **Christianity Explored** leader doesn't mean you have to live in a tent for ten weeks but, in order to be dedicated to individual participants, you will need to be dedicated in two particular areas:

1. dedicated to the Bible
2. dedicated to prayer

---

[2] Tertullian, *Address to the Martyrs*, Part 3. Taken from *The Epistle of the Gallican Churches Lugdunum and Vienna. With an appendix containing Tertullian's Address to Martyrs* (trans. T. Herbert Bindley; London: SPCK, 1900), p. 55.

1. DEDICATED TO THE BIBLE

God's word is where the power is. Whatever his personal circumstances, Paul knew that if the word were preached, it would do its work: "...I am suffering even to the point of being chained like a criminal. But God's word is not chained" (2 Timothy 2:9). In 2 Timothy 2:15, Paul exhorts Timothy to devote himself to the study of God's word: "Do your best to present yourself to God as one approved, a workman who does not need to be ashamed and who correctly handles the word of truth."

Because we're convinced of the power of God's word, every participant is given a Bible of their own at the beginning of the course, and our focus as leaders should consistently be on the Bible, specifically Mark's Gospel.

It is vital that you study Mark for yourself and think about its application in your own life. If the message of the Bible excites you, it will be exciting for those who attend the course.

2. DEDICATED TO PRAYER

Prayer is essential before, during and after the course. Paul opens his letter to Timothy by saying, "night and day I constantly remember you in my prayers" (2 Timothy 1:3). We, too, need to be constantly remembering the participants and our fellow leaders in our prayers.

Being dedicated to the Bible and prayer means being single-minded. As 2 Timothy 2:4 says, "No-one serving as a soldier gets involved in civilian affairs – he wants to please his commanding officer." Because the work of evangelism is so important, we must be ruthless in organizing our schedules to that end. The course will have a huge impact on our time.

Again and again, as we seek to make time to lead, to study Mark, to pray and to meet up with participants, the good will be the enemy of the best and the urgent will be the enemy of the important. We may find temptations or feelings of inadequacy creeping in. Sometimes, leading will be a real struggle: physically, emotionally and spiritually. After all, our enemy Satan hates the work we are doing.

But as Paul's illustration of the soldier makes clear, we must remain dedicated. If people stop attending, we keep praying for them. If they don't seem interested in the discussions, we keep studying and teaching Mark. We must not be discouraged, because we do it all for our "commanding officer," the Lord Jesus Christ.

BEFORE
THE COURSE

Before the course starts, there are a number of things you should do:

INVITE PEOPLE!

Ask people to be your guests at events organized by your church during which there will be an invitation by the speaker to attend *Christianity Explored*.

Or it may be appropriate to invite people directly to the course, letting them know that they will be able to ask any questions they want and that they will not be asked to pray, sing or read aloud. When inviting people to events or to *Christianity Explored*, it is important to be honest about exactly what will happen and who will be there.

While some people will respond positively to the first invitation they receive, for others it may take months or even years of working towards that point. Don't be discouraged if people don't respond right away.

READ MARK AND FAMILIARIZE YOURSELF WITH THE STUDY GUIDE SECTION OF THIS BOOK

You will feel much more confident to lead participants once you've prepared yourself for the Bible studies that make up *Christianity Explored*.

GET TO KNOW YOUR FELLOW LEADERS

Your course leader will probably have placed you in a team of three leaders. As a team, you will be praying, studying and teaching participants together, so it's important to get to know each other before you begin.

PREPARE YOUR TESTIMONY

"Always be prepared to give an answer to everyone who asks you to give the reason for the hope that you have. But do this with gentleness and respect..." (1 Peter 3:15).

A testimony is an honest and accurate account of God's work in your life. Everybody who has been born again and who is becoming like Christ has a unique, interesting and powerful testimony, regardless of whether or not it appears spectacular.

At some point during the course, you may feel it appropriate to share your testimony with the participants. Often someone will ask you directly how you became a Christian and you will need to have an answer ready.

You may find the guidelines below helpful as you prepare your testimony:

Keep it honest, personal and interesting

Tip: Your first sentence should make people sit up and listen. Anything too general, for example: "Well, I was brought up in a Christian home..." may make people switch off immediately.

Keep it short

Tip: Any more than three minutes may stretch people's patience. They can always ask you questions if they want to know more.

Keep pointing to Christ, not yourself

Tip: Your testimony is a great opportunity to communicate the gospel. Always include what it is that you believe, as well as how you came to believe it. As a general guide, try to explain why you think Jesus is God, how his death affects you personally, and what changes you have made in your life as a result.

> *Prepare your testimony. You might find it useful to share your testimony with other leaders and obtain feedback.*

I first came to faith at 14 having met a Christian Outreach team. Went home on a high to have my parents saying I should not get in too deep. Continued attending church wherever I went. When I was 16 I went to live with my grandmother who had a real living faith. I continued to attend church & joined the church there. When I was 19 I went to Lewis and stopped attending church because it was in Gaelic. After that I attended a Methodist church in Girvan. Really seeking the Lord. Went to Oban and stopped attending church again. Married in 1966 Back to church again. Moved to Lossiemouth stayed in church life. Moved to Alness & stayed in church. When G. Knuckles came to Alness he was so sure of his faith that I truly understood for the first time clearly that God was very personal. Since then my walk is still going on. Now I need to be with Christians. The world & materialism do not matter so much.

- that God would enable you to prepare well
- that the people you (and others) invite will attend the course
- that God would open the blind eyes of those who attend
- for the logistics of organizing the course
- for other leaders

We should be open and honest about how we can pray for one another during **Christianity Explored**.

➤ *Fill in the table below to help you pray for one another.*

Leader's Name	Prayer Points
1. Hugh	well prepared. Able to speak clearly
Jonathan	Be disciplined. Because of time. Organised. Not to feel guilty. Be able to accomplish things quickly. not to waffle.
2. Ronald	Concentration.
Agnes	Not to feel guilty · about not having fancy words.
3. Kathleen	Think first. Family not resentful
Mark	Focused on God. Remain steadfast. Concentration

➤ *Take time to pray now for the course, for your fellow leaders and for those you're thinking of inviting.*

DURING THE COURSE

The first two chapters of 1 Thessalonians give us a glimpse of the way in which Paul – and the others with him – preached the gospel. They are a useful guide as we seek to relate the gospel to those who participate in the course.

➤ *Read 1 Thessalonians chapters 1–2.*

Our hope as we run the course – which is the same hope Paul had as he preached – is that people will understand their need of rescue and turn to "serve the living and true God" (1 Thessalonians 1:9).

In order for that to happen, each part of the evening is important:

6:30 p.m.	**Leaders' prayer meeting**
7:00 p.m.	**Participants arrive for the meal**
7:45 p.m.	**GROUP DISCUSSION 1**
8:05 p.m.	**Talk / Video**
8:30 p.m.	**GROUP DISCUSSION 2**
9:00 p.m.	**End of the evening – "One-to-One"**

Note: All times are approximate. You can make certain sessions shorter or longer depending on your circumstances.

6:30 P.M. LEADERS' PRAYER MEETING

Each week, you and your fellow leaders may arrive having had a difficult time at home or at work. Many leaders find themselves coming under spiritual attack as they seek to serve God faithfully. So it is vital to begin the evening by supporting one another in prayer. It may be helpful to focus on a few Bible verses. It is also crucial to pray for the participants. Pray that the gospel will come to them "not simply with words, but also with power, with the Holy Spirit and with deep conviction" (1 Thessalonians 1:5).

7:00 P.M. MEAL

Having prayed together as leaders, you are ready to welcome the participants as they begin to arrive for the meal. Make a point of learning their names in Week 1. Being greeted by name by a leader in the second week will mean a great deal to participants.

Paul wrote, "We loved you so much that we were delighted to share with you not only the gospel of God but our lives as well, because you had become so dear to us" (1 Thessalonians 2:8). During the meal, it is important to share our lives with the participants. We want them to meet credible, open, caring Christians.

Try to avoid heavy theological discussions during this time. The intention is to share life, not to be spiritually intense. We need to remember that the participants have probably been treated as "human resources" all day. Our aim, by contrast, should be to celebrate them as human beings made in the image of God. We want people to be able to relax and, above all, to realize that we are interested in every aspect of their well-being, not just the spiritual. Find out about their hobbies, jobs, families, holidays, culture and interests.

7:45 P.M. GROUP DISCUSSION 1

This discussion has two components. First, groups discuss any issues arising from the previous week's HOME STUDY (this HOME STUDY involves reading a few chapters from the Bible and answering questions). Second, groups look together at a passage from the Bible.

➤ *Please see pages 69 – 70 for an example of this.*

CHRISTIANITY
E⅄PLORED

Since not everyone will have done his or her HOME STUDY every week, it's important not to make anyone feel uncomfortable. If nobody has anything they'd like to discuss, move on to the Bible passage for that week. (The passage is always taken from the section participants should have read for their HOME STUDY anyway.)

As Christians, we are entrusted with the gospel, and that means we must present it clearly. We're not presenting our own personal agendas, and we're not seeking to dupe anyone into becoming a Christian. We want participants to be able to make an informed decision about Christ. "For the appeal we make does not spring from error or impure motives, nor are we trying to trick you. On the contrary, we speak as men approved by God to be entrusted with the gospel" (1 Thessalonians 2:3–4).

During GROUP DISCUSSION 1 you may get replies that approach the answer to a question but are not quite complete. Try to guide participants from these initial answers to a better, more biblical answer.

- Have further questions in mind to develop the initial answer, for example: "What did you mean by that?" "What does everyone else think?" "Where does it say that?"

- If someone gives a wrong answer, it may be tempting to correct them immediately. Instead, try opening up the discussion by asking others what they think, for example: "Does everyone agree with Jane?"

- Don't be afraid to correct a wrong answer graciously if you think the answer will take the group too far "off topic," for example: "Thank you John, that's an interesting point, but I'm not sure that's what's going on here."

Sometimes, individual personalities may make it difficult to conduct an effective group discussion:

- "Silent Sue" – never contributes to the discussion. She's best helped by encouraging people to work through questions in groups of two or three at points during the study and then having them feed their answers back to the main group.

- "Talkative Tim" – likes to monopolize the discussion. Depending on how well you know him, either subdivide the group into smaller groups to give others an opportunity to speak, or have a quiet and tactful word with him (for example: "Tim, thanks so much for everything you're contributing. I wonder if you could help me with the quieter members of the group...")

- "Angry Andy" – attacks the answers given by everyone else in the group. It's best to take him aside at the end of the evening and listen to any specific issues he may have. If the problem persists, it may be appropriate to remove Andy from the group, asking him to meet with you "one-to-one" at a different time.

- "Know-It-All Nick" – immediately answers every question, thus stifling the group. This situation is best dealt with by supplementary questions to facilitate group discussion (for example: "Does everyone agree with Nick?").

- "Off-On-A-Tangent Ollie" – loves to steer the discussion away from the topic and talk about something entirely different. It may be that this new subject is something the whole group wants to explore, but if not, tactfully suggest that it might be good to discuss it more fully at the end of the evening.

8:05 P.M. TALK / VIDEO

At this point in the evening, the course leader presents a talk (or a video is shown).

If you've heard the talks – or watched the videos – before, it can be tempting to switch off and stop listening, but bear in mind that if you don't listen, participants won't either.

8:30 P.M. GROUP DISCUSSION 2

Use the questions to encourage discussion as you explore together the truths that have been presented.

➤ Please see page 71 for an example of this.

Having spent a while listening, it's important that participants now feel able to speak freely. Although there will be opportunities to teach, the leader's primary role in this group discussion is therefore to listen and to ensure that everyone is heard. "But we were gentle among you, like a mother caring for her little children" (1 Thessalonians 2:7).

- Leaders should try to avoid speaking immediately after each other.

- You may feel it is appropriate to "carry over" a discussion from GROUP DISCUSSION 1, if you were unable to adequately cover an important issue.

- Be gracious and courteous, and act as peacemaker if the discussion gets heated.

- If a question is met with silence, don't be too quick to interject. Allow people time to think.

- It may be appropriate in certain circumstances to address a question directly to a participant in order to encourage discussion (for example: "Sam, what do you think about this?")

- If one person's particular issue begins to dominate, gently ask him or her if you can talk about the issue together at the end of the session.

- Don't forget how important the tone of your voice and your body language can be as you seek to further the discussion.

- Lead honestly. You won't be able to deal with all the questions thrown your way, so don't pretend to have all the answers. Some questions can be easily addressed, but others will be difficult. If you don't know the answer, say so – but try to have an answer ready for the following week.

9:00 P.M. END OF THE EVENING – "ONE-TO-ONE"

As the course leader brings the evening to a formal close, you should direct participants to complete the HOME STUDY in their *Study Guide* before the following week. Invite them to stay a while longer if they'd like to chat things through, but make it clear that they are free to go – as promised – at 9 p.m. This is another small way of earning people's trust.

It is at this point that the most effective conversations take place, because you have time to talk "one-to-one" with participants. "For you know that we dealt with each of you as a father deals with his own children, encouraging, comforting and urging you to live lives worthy of God" (1 Thessalonians 2:11–12).

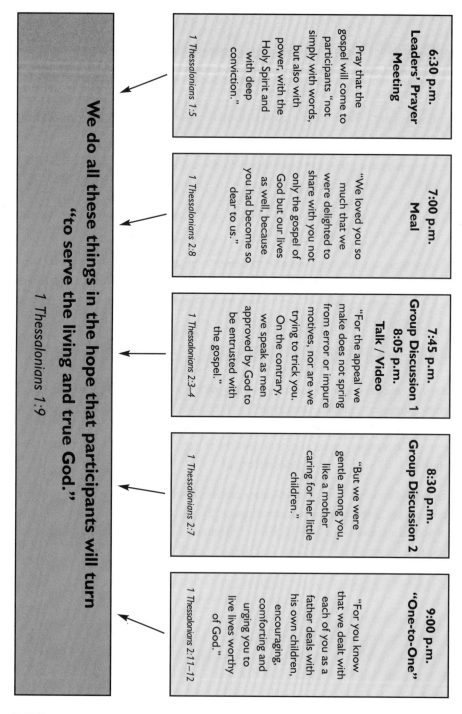

**6:30 p.m.
Leaders' Prayer
Meeting**

Pray that the gospel will come to participants "not simply with words, but also with power, with the Holy Spirit and with deep conviction."

1 Thessalonians 1:5

**7:00 p.m.
Meal**

"We loved you so much that we were delighted to share with you not only the gospel of God but our lives as well, because you had become so dear to us."

1 Thessalonians 2:8

**7:45 p.m.
Group Discussion 1
8:05 p.m.
Talk / Video**

"For the appeal we make does not spring from error or impure motives, nor are we trying to trick you. On the contrary, we speak as men approved by God to be entrusted with the gospel."

1 Thessalonians 2:3–4

**8:30 p.m.
Group Discussion 2**

"But we were gentle among you, like a mother caring for her little children."

1 Thessalonians 2:7

**9:00 p.m.
"One-to-One"**

"For you know that we dealt with each of you as a father deals with his own children, encouraging, comforting and urging you to live lives worthy of God."

1 Thessalonians 2:11–12

We do all these things in the hope that participants will turn "to serve the living and true God."

1 Thessalonians 1:9

CHRISTIANITY
EXPLORED

EXPLORE, EXPLAIN, ENCOURAGE

"Explore, Explain, Encourage" is a useful way of remembering how we should lead *Christianity Explored*. First we **explore** what issues are important to participants, then we seek to **explain** the Bible in a way that is relevant to those issues, and lastly we **encourage** participants to act on the truths they've discovered.

1. EXPLORE

In his letter, James writes, "My dear brothers, take note of this: Everyone should be quick to listen, slow to speak and slow to become angry..." (James 1:19).

The conversation in your group should be like the conversation at a dinner party.

You, as the host, are encouraging your guests to relax, feel comfortable and express their thoughts and ideas. Participants must see that their views are taken seriously and not dismissed, so take time to explore what is important to them.

Leaders should listen very carefully to participants, to find out how they think and why. What is their most pressing issue? It might be how a loving God could have allowed the death of a family member, or the loss of a long-term job. It might be resentment at the idea that God has something to say about who they are and the way they live their life.

Bear in mind that the questions participants raise may subtly indicate more fundamental objections to Christianity. For instance, if someone seems to have a problem believing that Jonah could have survived in a giant fish for three days, you could give many detailed examples of the regurgitation of human beings by large aquatic creatures. However, it might be wiser to see that the participant's real issue is probably with the general trustworthiness of the Bible, and deal with that.

Next we need to ask ourselves, "Which part of the gospel is most relevant to this person?" Now that we know what some of their questions and issues are, what do we need to explain to them?

That's where *Two Ways to Live*[3] comes in. In six simple stages, this diagram outlines what the Bible has to say about our relationship with God, and what Jesus has to do with that relationship. You can find it on the next page.

➤ *Please learn* Two Ways to Live, *then try presenting it to another leader.*

---

[3] © Phillip Jensen 1989, 1993, *Two Ways to Live* booklets and training material published by Matthias Media/The Good Book Company, London.

1

God is the loving ruler of the world.
He made the world.
He made us rulers of the world under him.

You are worthy, our Lord and God,
to receive glory and honour and power,
for you created all things, and by your will
they were created and have their being.
Revelation 4:11

But is that the way it is now?

2

We all reject the ruler – God – by trying
to run life our own way without him.
(This is what the Bible calls "sin.")
But we fail to rule ourselves or society
or the world.

There is no-one righteous, not even one;
there is no-one who understands,
no-one who seeks God. All have turned away.
Romans 3:10–12

What will God do about this rebellion?

3

God won't let us rebel forever.
God's punishment for rebellion is
death and judgement.

Man is destined to die once,
and after that to face judgement.
Hebrews 9:27

God's justice sounds hard. But...

4

Because of his love, God sent his Son into the
world: the man Jesus Christ. Jesus always lived
under God's rule: he did nothing that deserved
death or judgement. But Jesus died in order
to take the punishment that we deserve.
He died in our place, to bring us forgiveness.

Christ died for sins once for all, the righteous
for the unrighteous, to bring you to God.
1 Peter 3:18

And that's not all...

5

God raised Jesus to life again as the ruler of
the world. Jesus has conquered death, offers
eternal life, and will return to judge.

In his great mercy he has given us new birth
into a living hope through the resurrection of
Jesus Christ from the dead.
1 Peter 1:3

Where does that leave us?

6 There are two ways to live:

Our way: Reject the ruler – God.
Try to run life our own way.

Result: Condemned by God.
Facing death and judgement.

God's way: Submit to Jesus as our ruler.
Trust in Jesus' death and
resurrection.

Result: Forgiven by God.
Given eternal life.

Whoever believes in the Son has eternal life,
but whoever rejects the Son will not see life,
for God's wrath remains on him.
John 3:36

Which way do you want to live?

Two Ways to Live is useful in many different situations. Once you've identified a participant's most pressing issue, think about which of the six boxes would be most helpful for that person to understand. Explain that part of the gospel to them first, and then, if appropriate, explain how that part fits into the gospel as a whole.

➤ *In the space below, decide which box you would start with if the pressing issue was…*

…believing that God could love them.

➤ *In the space below, decide which box you would start with if the pressing issue was…*

…what will happen to them when they die.

➤ *In the space below, decide which box you would start with if the pressing issue was…*

…why God allows suffering.

There are different ways of approaching each of these three issues. For the first, you might start with box 4, and help them to understand the significance of Jesus' death on the cross.

One way of approaching the second issue is to start with box 3. Explain that after death there will be a judgement. Then you might jump to box 6 and show that the answer to their question depends on their response to God.

One way of tackling the third is to start by explaining box 2. Explain what "sin" is, and that it is the root cause of human suffering. You may then want to point them to Genesis 3 and explain that we live in a cursed world. Then you could take them

CHRISTIANITY
E✝PLORED

to Romans 8:18–25, which explains that all suffering will eventually come to an end. The person leading with you might then bring in box 4, explaining that God himself knows what it is to suffer, and that he watched his own Son murdered by those he came to rescue.

> *Think of an unbelieving friend that you know well. Consider that person's pressing issues and write them in the box below.*

> *Now decide which of the boxes you might start with as you help them to understand the gospel.*

Sometimes – perhaps during a "One-to-One" session – it might be appropriate to take a participant through *Two Ways to Live* in its entirety. For example, if a participant asks, "What exactly do Christians believe?" you can sketch out the boxes on a piece of paper in a few minutes. You can then follow up your answer by asking them which of the boxes they struggle to believe.

Two Ways to Live can also be used if a person wants to make a commitment to Christ. Again, sketch it out in its entirety and then take participants through the "a, b, c, d":

a – Do you **accept** you've sinned?   (box 2)

b – Do you **believe** Christ died for you?   (box 4)

c – Have you **counted the cost**?   (box 6)

d – **Do it**. Put your trust in Christ.   (box 6)

3. ENCOURAGE

Lastly, as well as exploring and explaining, we need to encourage those in our care.

Encouragement is vital to those who are starting to grasp the truth of Christianity. Acting on these truths is no easy task, because it will entail the "obedience that comes from faith" (Romans 1:5).

Don't underestimate how encouraging your own testimony can be in this context. When you openly share with others your own struggle to trust and obey Jesus, it helps those in your group to feel that they're not alone. We shouldn't pretend that we always find it easy to pray, to read the Bible, to change much-loved habits. So don't be afraid to show that you're human too. (However, this should never be at the expense of listening to *their* struggles, and it is obviously not an excuse to celebrate how sinful we can be!)

Paul tells us that as believers we have been given the "light of the knowledge of the glory of God in the face of Christ" (2 Corinthians 4:6). But he continues, "we have this treasure in jars of clay to show that this all-surpassing power is from God and not from us" (2 Corinthians 4:7). Sometimes we think we need to appear morally flawless and supernaturally wise if we're to win a hearing for Christ. But it is actually only when we are weak – when we show our dependence on God's strength – that he is glorified, and others are drawn to him.

IDENTITY,
MISSION, CALL

As a leader preparing to teach Mark, there's no substitute for reading through Mark's Gospel at least two or three times.

And as you read, you'll begin to see that Mark is preoccupied with three great themes:

• Who was Jesus? (Jesus' **identity**)

• Why did he come? (Jesus' **mission**)

• What does he require of his followers? (Jesus' **call**)

IDENTITY, MISSION, CALL IN MARK 8

By way of an example, look at one of the most significant passages in Mark's Gospel – Mark chapter 8 verses 27 to 38 – and you'll discover all three themes in quick succession. Let's take a few verses at a time.

➤ *Read Mark 8:27–30.*

The dominant question in verses 27–30 is Jesus' **identity**. Who exactly was Jesus?

People had lots of theories, just as they do now: "Some say John the Baptist; others say Elijah; and still others, one of the prophets." But Jesus gets very personal in verse 29: "What about you? ... Who do you say I am?"

Peter answers the question concerning Jesus' identity correctly: "You are the Christ." He is not "one of the prophets" as some were saying, he is actually the Christ: the fulfillment of all prophecy.

➤ *Read Mark 8:31–33.*

But although Peter has Jesus' identity right, it's clear he hasn't yet understood Jesus' **mission**.

Here, for the first time, Jesus begins to teach that he "must suffer many things and be rejected by the elders, chief priests and teachers of the law, and that he must be killed and after three days rise again."

Jesus doesn't leave any room for misunderstanding (he "spoke plainly about this") because he knows that the disciples – and most of the public – have a very different idea of what the Christ would be like. He would be a triumphant king, marching in to claim his territory, trampling the enemy underfoot and ushering in a glorious new era for his followers. A Christ who suffered and died would have seemed like a contradiction in terms.

Peter clearly has this triumphal view of the Christ in mind when he takes Jesus aside and begins "to rebuke him." But Jesus' strong reaction shows just how necessary death is to his mission: "Get behind me, Satan! ... You do not have in mind the things of God, but the things of men."

The idea that the so-called "Son of God" had to suffer and die is still a stumbling block for many people today. But if we're to understand Mark's Gospel – and indeed the whole Bible – correctly, it is essential to grasp the true nature of Jesus' mission: he "must suffer" and "he must be killed" so that we can be forgiven.

➤ Read Mark 8:34–38.

If that is what Jesus came to do, what are the implications for his followers? What is Christ's **call**?

Having just spoken to the disciples about his own death, he calls the crowd to him and says, "If anyone would come after me, he must deny himself and take up his cross and follow me." It is striking, and not a little disturbing, to see Jesus immediately turn his attention from the cross he must take up, to the cross we must take up.

Firstly, if we are to follow him, Jesus tells us we must deny ourselves. It is not a natural thing for human beings to turn away from their natural self-centeredness and self-reliance, but that is Jesus' call. We cannot follow him unless we deny our own selfish instincts.

Second, we cannot follow Jesus if we are not prepared to take up our cross. We must be prepared to serve him – and others – to the point of giving up our lives. In effect, Jesus must be more important to us than life itself.

If that seems irrational, we need to hear what Jesus says next: "For whoever wants to save his life will lose it, but whoever loses his life for me and for the gospel will save it." Just as Jesus took up his cross, died and was resurrected, so we – if we obey his call – will die to our old lives and discover a new life far surpassing anything we have previously known.

So that's identity, mission and call in Mark 8.

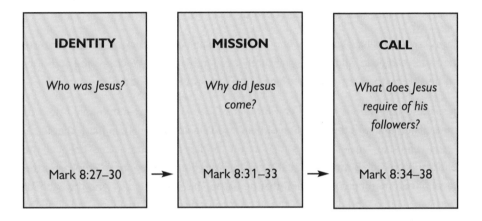

IDENTITY	MISSION	CALL
Who was Jesus?	Why did Jesus come?	What does Jesus require of his followers?
Mark 8:27–30	Mark 8:31–33	Mark 8:34–38

Now, let's look briefly at those themes as they appear throughout Mark.

"IDENTITY" IN MARK'S GOSPEL

Broadly speaking, the first half of Mark (1:1–8:29) is taken up with the question of Jesus' identity: it starts by saying, "The beginning of the gospel about Jesus Christ, the Son of God" and ends with Peter's statement, "You are the Christ."

➤ Read Isaiah 35:4–6.

Through the prophet Isaiah, God told his people how they would recognize the Christ, his anointed King, when he came: the deaf will hear, the blind will see, the lame will walk and the mute will speak.

Among many other miracles recorded in the first half of Mark's Gospel, Jesus makes a lame man walk in chapter 2, he makes a deaf and mute man hear and speak in chapter 7, and he enables a blind man to see in chapter 8. Jesus demonstrates his power in this specific way so that people will recognize him as the Christ.

➤ Read Mark 1:2–3.

The second half of the quotation is from Isaiah 40, a passage that makes it clear that this "Lord" who is mentioned is none other than God himself, the one who miraculously delivered his people from Egypt, the creator of the world. Mark tells us that John the Baptist is the "voice of one calling in the desert" who will prepare the way for the Lord. When John baptizes Jesus, the voice from heaven confirms that Jesus is indeed the promised Lord of Isaiah 40.

Jesus certainly behaves as if he were God himself: he heals the sick, he controls nature, he raises the dead, and most significantly of all in Mark 2:5, he claims the authority to be able to forgive sin – something only God (as the offended party) can do.

Jesus also talks about himself as if he were God. Jesus most commonly refers to himself in Mark with the title "Son of Man" (see Daniel 7:13–14). In Mark chapter 2, Jesus refers to himself in verse 19 as the bridegroom, and as the Lord of the Sabbath in verse 28. (In Hosea, God calls himself the bridegroom to emphasize the level of commitment and passion that he has for his people Israel. And the Sabbath was a festival to God during which the Jews remembered all that God had done for them.) Perhaps the clearest reference to Jesus' divinity is in Mark 6:50, where Jesus takes the precious covenant name of God – Yahweh (a Hebrew name meaning "I am") – and uses it of himself: "Take courage! It is I" ("Yahweh" in the original).

To speak as Jesus spoke is blasphemy – unless, of course, you really are God.

This is not to say that all the evidence concerning Jesus' identity comes from the first half of Mark's Gospel. Indeed, the crowning proof of all that we have said about Jesus' identity is his resurrection from the dead (16:6).

"MISSION" IN MARK'S GOSPEL

If Mark is telling us anything about humanity, it's that we desperately need to be saved. Jesus tells us in Mark 12:30–31 that the greatest commandment is this: "Love the Lord your God with all your heart and with all your soul and with all your mind

CHRISTIANITY
E✝PLORED

and with all your strength." And the second greatest is to "Love your neighbour as yourself." But all of us know that we haven't lived like that. So, if we're to avoid God's just condemnation, we desperately need to be rescued.

In fact, Jesus says, our hearts are evil: "out of men's hearts, come evil thoughts, sexual immorality, theft, murder, adultery, greed, malice, deceit, lewdness, envy, slander, arrogance and folly. All these evils come from inside and make a man 'unclean'" (Mark 7:21–23). In other words, we are sinful.

Mark chapter 10 makes it clear that we are unable to save ourselves from this predicament. First, in verses 1 to 12, we're told that even the Old Testament law, which the Pharisees cherished so much, is unable to solve the problem of sin. It was precisely because of people's sin that Moses allowed divorce in some circumstances (10:5), even though divorce was never something God intended (10:6–9).

Then, in 10:17, we meet the rich young man. He comes to Jesus asking, "what must I do to inherit eternal life?" The point, of course, is that there is nothing he can "do" to earn salvation for himself. Like all of us, his heart is fundamentally – and mortally – flawed. Even this rich young man – this respectful, intelligent, wealthy, moral, religious man – is unable to save himself by his own efforts. "Who then can be saved?" the disciples ask, amazed. Jesus responds, "With man this is impossible, but not with God; all things are possible with God" (10:27).

So we're left with a question: how does God deal with the problem of our sin? The answer comes in one of the most famous verses of Mark's Gospel, chapter 10, verse 45: "For even the Son of Man did not come to be served, but to serve, and to give his life as a ransom for many."

The way that God will rescue us from our sin is by sending his Son to die for us as "a ransom." In dying, Jesus will bear God's just punishment for our sin. It is the only way that we human beings can be restored to the perfect relationship with God for which we were designed. Our hearts are so evil (Mark 7:21–23) that nothing less than the death of God incarnate, Jesus Christ, will work.

This, then, is Jesus' mission: he *must* die so that sinful people can be rescued (Mark 8:31; 9:12, 31; 10:33, 45). The second half of Mark's Gospel is dominated by the cross, because – as we've seen – Jesus' death is central to his mission.

Jesus says this to prospective followers: "If anyone would come after me, he must deny himself and take up his cross and follow me" (Mark 8:34).

As we've seen, that means turning away from our instinctive self-centeredness and being prepared to give up our lives for Jesus.

Just in case we think that following Jesus sounds like a bad deal, verses 35–38 of chapter 8 give us four very good reasons to do just that:

• If we give up our life for him, we'll save it; and if we don't, we'll lose it (v. 35).

• If by rejecting Jesus we gain the whole world, we still lose the most important thing we have (v. 36).

• If we miss out on eternal life, there's nothing we can do to buy it back (v. 37).

• If we reject Jesus, then he will reject us when he returns as judge of the world (v. 38).

Jesus' role as judge of the world is an undercurrent that runs throughout Mark, and we must remember that Jesus will be our judge when considering how to respond to Jesus' call.

Even as far back as Mark 1:2, we're reminded that Jesus is the judge. Just before the quotation from Isaiah in verse 3 comes a phrase from Malachi 3:1 – "I will send my messenger ahead of you, who will prepare your way." As we've seen, the way is being prepared for "the Lord." And, as chapters 3 and 4 of Malachi make clear in no uncertain terms, this Lord is coming to judge.

Jesus certainly acts as judge. For example, the Jewish establishment consider him a blasphemer (2:7), they question his actions (2:16, 24), they harden their hearts against him (3:5) and, by Mark 3:6, they are already beginning to plot "how they might kill Jesus." And Jesus' first act of judgement against them immediately follows: "Jesus withdrew with his disciples to the lake." The word translated "withdrew" is a strong, striking word. It means that he is deliberately turning his back on them.

Nevertheless, their opposition to Jesus continues. In 3:22, they say that the only reason he's able to drive out demons is because he himself is possessed by the devil. In 8:11, they start trying to test him. They test him again in 10:2. And again in 12:13. Eventually, they pay Judas to betray him to his death.

What we read in 11:13–14 shows that there will come a time when it will no longer be possible for the Jewish authorities – or anyone else – to repent. The warnings will cease, and a final judgement will fall. Jesus walks up to a fig-tree that is in leaf, hoping to find fruit on it. But when he gets there, he finds that although the tree looks good from a distance, it has no fruit. So, in verse 14, Jesus curses the tree: "May no-one ever eat fruit from you again." If you read on to verse 20, you'll see that the fig-tree had completely withered, right from the roots.

So why does Mark put verses 15 to 19 (Jesus overturning the tables in the temple) between verse 14 and verse 20? It's because the episode with the fig-tree helps us understand what's going on in the temple.

Just like the fig-tree, the temple promises good fruit from a distance. Jesus arrives at the temple, hoping to find the fruit of godliness, because it is meant to be "a house of prayer for all nations" (v.17). Instead, Jesus finds "a den of robbers." So he overturns the merchants' tables as a symbolic act of his judgement on the temple.

And in 8:38 Jesus makes it clear that judgement will not be limited to the Jewish authorities: "If anyone is ashamed of me and my words in this adulterous and sinful generation, the Son of Man will be ashamed of him when he comes in his Father's glory with the holy angels." When Jesus comes again, he will judge anyone and everyone who has gone through life ignoring him and his call.

THE IMPORTANCE OF IDENTITY, MISSION, CALL

A participant's understanding of Jesus' identity, mission *and* call is crucial to the way in which he or she will respond to the gospel.

➤ *Write down what you think the problems might be for a person who has understood:*

Jesus' identity and mission but **not** his call

Nominal Christian who stops short of making a commitment

Jesus' identity and call but not his mission

They don't realise that they need to be rescued. They would be offended. They won't know the joy of forgiveness.

Jesus' mission and call but not his identity

would not understand his mission or call if they did not know who he was. A universal type who thinks all religions lead to the same thing.

There are a number of implications that arise in each instance. For example:

If a person understands Jesus' identity and mission, but not his call, they won't understand the need to deny themselves or take up their cross. As a result, their lives won't be changed and, because any suffering they face will be unexpected, they are likely to become disillusioned and turn away from Christianity.

CHRISTIANITY
EXPLORED

If a person understands Jesus' identity and call, but not his mission, they won't understand the seriousness of their sin or the fact that Jesus has paid the price for it. As a result, they won't know the joy of forgiveness. Because they have not understood what grace means, their life will become a dutiful and "religious" dirge.

They will either become self-righteous or become paralyzed by their sense of failure. Because they have not understood the cross, they can have no assurance of heaven. Failure to understand the seriousness of sin is likely to leave them hugely discouraged by the evil they see in the world.

If a person understands Jesus' mission and call, but not his identity, they won't understand that Jesus is God. As a result, they will see Jesus merely as an example of how one might live. There will be no consistent motivation to live the Christian life. They won't know that God loves them or that God is sovereign over their life.

➤ *Think about how you became a Christian and write down your answers to the following: When did you first understand who Jesus was? When did you understand why he came? At what point did you realize what Jesus demands of you?*

Knew as a child that Jesus was god's son.

➤ Look through Mark's Gospel and decide what each paragraph has to say about Jesus' identity, mission or call. Label each one "I," "M" or "C," remembering that some paragraphs may be a combination of two or three of the above.

SESSION 8

AFTER
THE COURSE

Christianity Explored is not a ten-week conveyor belt that either ships unbelievers into the Christian faith – or tips them off into the street outside. It is therefore vital to have a coherent follow-up strategy in place for all participants.

GIVE OUT FEEDBACK FORMS

Feedback forms, given out during the last week of the course, are a great way to challenge course participants to think about where they currently are with Christ, and to help leaders plan a way forward once the course is ended. You can find a sample feedback form in the book *How To Run The Course*.

STAY IN TOUCH

Having spent ten weeks with your group considering profound and personal issues, you will know them well – and they will know you well. Under these circumstances, it would clearly be wrong to "drop" participants once the course comes to an end. Whatever their response has been, God has not given up on them, and neither should you. Furthermore, if the friends who invited these people along see leaders maintaining a genuine interest in the participants, they will feel more confident about bringing others along in future. Plan to stay in touch with all the members of your group, and arrange it with your co-leaders so that each participant has at least one Christian who remains in touch with him or her.

ARRANGE FOLLOW-UP FOR NEW BELIEVERS

If anyone in your group has made a commitment to Christ, it's vital to help them lay firm foundations so that they will be able to persevere. Invite them to start coming along to church with you if they're not already regularly attending. It is often a difficult task to get people into the habit of meeting together regularly on a Sunday, but the concept of a Christian who doesn't go to church is foreign to the New Testament, so help them to take this seriously (Hebrews 10:25). Introduce them to other Christians and encourage them to become integrated within the church by joining a Bible study group and finding an area of service within which they can participate.

ARRANGE FOLLOW-UP FOR THOSE WHO HAVEN'T YET MADE A COMMITMENT

Don't be disheartened if people have not made a commitment during the course. Bear in mind the parable of the growing seed in Mark 4:26–29, which shows that good things come to those who wait. Ask whether they are interested in exploring Christianity further. If they are, one option is to invite them to come back and go through *Christianity Explored* again – some people have gone through the course three or more times before they felt ready to make a commitment. Remember that they aren't just re-hearing the talks but re-reading Mark's Gospel as well, which will work on their hearts each time it is opened.

RECOMMEND OR GIVE AWAY BOOKS

Reading a good Christian book at the right time can be very influential. Think carefully about the books you have read and see if any of them would suit particular members of your group. If you're not an avid reader, ask around for advice about books suitable for people in different situations.[4]

---

[4] The *Christianity Explored* website lists a number of recommended books on various subjects. Visit the "Running a Course" section at www.christianityexplored.com

READ THE BIBLE WITH A PARTICIPANT

You might suggest getting together with an individual on a regular basis to read through a book of the Bible. This can be totally informal; just two friends with an open Bible finding out what God's word has to say to them.

Questions to guide your study could be:

What does the passage mean?
Are there any difficult words or ideas that merit special attention?

What does the passage mean in context?
What comes before / after the passage? Why is the passage placed where it is? Is it addressed to a specific individual or group of people? Why?

What does the passage mean for us?
What have we learned about ourselves? About God? How do we apply the passage to our lives?

PRAY

A supremely Christ-like way of caring for people is to pray for them. Even after the course has ended, it is important to pray for all the members of the group. For new believers, pray for growth, fruitfulness and joy. For those who have not yet made a commitment, pray that the Lord will have mercy on them and send his Holy Spirit to open their blind eyes to see who Jesus is. Pray for yourself, for patience and wisdom as you wait for God's word to do its work.

➤ *After the course has ended, use this space to write down how you intend to support the participants in your care.*

GETTING OUR EXPECTATIONS RIGHT

Jesus was the most brilliant teacher who ever lived. Nevertheless, a glance through Mark chapter 3 reminds us that:

- those in authority wanted him dead (v. 6)
- the public were often more interested in his miracles than in his teaching (vv. 9–10)
- one of his own followers was eventually to betray him (v. 19)
- his own family thought he was out of his mind (v. 21)
- many religious people thought he was evil (v. 22)

Yet, in spite of all this pressure, rather than change tack or water down his message, Jesus continued to teach: "With many similar parables Jesus spoke the word to them, as much as they could understand" (Mark 4:33).

We, too, will face pressure. So why should we persist in teaching God's word to people who don't seem to be listening, or who openly oppose us?

Jesus gives us the answer in Mark chapter 4: God's word produces dramatic results (vv. 8, 20, 32). But he begins by warning us to expect disappointment and delay.

EXPECT DISAPPOINTMENT

➤ *Read Mark 4:1–8, 14–20.*

The seed (which is "the word," as Jesus explains in v. 14) can fall in unfruitful places:

- along the path (v. 15)
- on rocky places (v. 16)
- among thorns (v. 18)

There will be those who delight us by turning up in the first week, but who never come again. There will be those who joyfully pray the prayer of commitment in Week 7 but, because of family pressure, they soon decide it's just not worth the trouble. Then there are those who diligently attend each week of the course but decide right at the end that their material possessions mean more to them than anything they've heard.

It can be desperately disappointing to see participants apparently respond to the gospel message, but then show no sign of lasting change. But Jesus warns us to expect it.

EXPECT DELAY

➤ *Read Mark 4:26–29.*

Jesus uses the metaphor of the seed with good reason: it takes time for seed to grow.

The farmer has to be patient: "Night and day, whether he sleeps or gets up, the seed sprouts and grows, though he does not know how" (Mark 4:27). He just has to trust that the seed will grow, even though it may seem that nothing much is happening.

We live in an instant culture – instant food, instant information, instant credit – and we may find ourselves expecting participants to acquire an instant relationship with God. But delay is as much a part of our work as it is the farmer's. We must be prepared to stay in touch with participants for weeks, months, or even years after the course ends.

There will be those who seem to agree with everything they learn through the course. You decide to meet up with them on a regular basis and, a year later, they still agree with everything they've learned. But they're not Christians.

There may be times when we lose patience and are tempted to give up. But we must continue to plant the word in people's lives, trusting in its power, and remembering that God's timescale is very different from our own.

CHRISTIANITY
EXPLORED

➤ *Read Mark 4:30–32.*

Despite the inevitable disappointments and delays, there is a good reason to continue sowing God's word in people's lives, just as Jesus did: "…when planted, it grows and becomes the largest of all garden plants, with such big branches that the birds of the air can perch in its shade" (Mark 4:32). Even a tiny seed – like the mustard seed – can produce dramatic results.

There will be those who bring up the same difficult issues week after week. Then suddenly one of those people will arrive one week and tell you he or she has become a Christian. A year later that person is a **Christianity Explored** leader, and a few months after that, that same person is applying to theological college in order to be able to teach the gospel more clearly to others.

As Jesus tells us in Mark 4:20, there will be those who hear the word, accept it, and then go on to "produce a crop – thirty, sixty or even a hundred times what was sown."

It is a great encouragement to remember that the power to change lives is not in our eloquence – it is in God's word. So we must continue to preach the word faithfully, whatever disappointments we suffer, whatever delays we endure, and whatever circumstances we face.

Notes

Notes

CHRISTIANITY E✝PLORED

SECTION 2
STUDY GUIDE

This section contains talk outlines and studies to work through over the ten-week course. It is an exact duplicate of the material in the participant's *Study Guide*, together with instructions for leaders, additional notes and the answers to each question.

- Don't worry if you don't have time to go through all of the questions with your group – the most important thing is to listen to the participants and answer their questions.

- Try to avoid using "jargon" that might alienate participants. Bear in mind that words and phrases familiar to Christians (for example, "pagan," "washed in the blood," "house group," "the Lord" and so on) may seem strange to those outside Christian circles.

- If participants miss a week, take time during the meal to summarize briefly what was taught the week before.

- Some participants may believe that the Bible is not reliable as a source of history. If this issue arises during a group discussion, refer them to the "Before We Begin" chapter on page 6 of their *Study Guide*. The table on page 8 of their guide (re-printed on page 60 of this guide) is a useful tool to establish the historical reliability of the New Testament.

➤ *The information below appears in the opening of the participant's* Study Guide *and is printed here for your reference, with additional footnotes.*

THE JOURNEY AHEAD

Welcome to **Christianity Explored**.

Over the next ten weeks, we will explore three questions that cut right to the heart of Christianity: Who was Jesus? Why did he come? What is involved in following him?

Don't be afraid to ask questions, no matter how simple or difficult you think they are. And if you have to miss a week, don't worry. You can always ask someone in your group for a quick summary of what you've missed.

So who was Jesus? Why did he come? And what does it mean to follow him?

OUR GUIDE, MARK

To help us answer those questions, we're going to use one of the books of the Bible. It's a book named after its author, Mark.

But before we start looking at the Bible, here are some tips on finding your way around it:

* The Bible is divided into two main sections: the Old Testament and the New Testament. The Old Testament was written before Jesus was born and the New Testament was written after Jesus was born.

* There are 66 books in the Bible: 39 in the Old Testament and 27 in the New Testament.

* Every Bible has a contents page at the front that will help you find the books referred to in this *Study Guide*.

CHRISTIANITY
EXPLORED

- Each book of the Bible is divided up into chapters and each chapter is further divided into individual verses, all of which are numbered. So "Mark 1:1 – 3:6" refers to the book of Mark, chapter 1, verse 1, through to chapter 3, verse 6. All the Bible references in this *Study Guide* are written in this way.

- There are four accounts of Jesus' life in the Bible, all named after their authors: Matthew, Mark, Luke and John. They're known as "Gospels" (the word "gospel" literally means "good news").

- You can find the book of Mark (also known as Mark's Gospel) about three-quarters of the way through your Bible, between the books of Matthew and Luke.

WHY SHOULD WE READ MARK'S GOSPEL?

One reason to read Mark is that his book is the shortest of the four Gospels!

Another reason is that Mark opens his book with a staggering claim. In his first sentence, Mark claims that Jesus Christ is "the Son of God" (Mark 1:1). In other words, Mark tells us that Jesus is God in human form.

By reading Mark, you have the opportunity to prove – or disprove – the writer's claim.

CAN WE RELY ON MARK'S GOSPEL?

You may be wondering whether Mark is a reliable place to find out about Jesus. So it's important to ask the same questions we should ask of any document that claims to record history:

What do we know about the author?

Mark was a close associate of Peter, who was one of Jesus' "apostles" (those who Jesus specifically called to be witnesses of his life; see Mark 3:14). Papias, writing in about AD 130, recorded the connection between Mark and Peter: "Mark being the interpreter of Peter, whatsoever he recorded he wrote with great accuracy."[1]

When was the document written?

Peter clearly knew he would soon be killed for his belief in Jesus and wrote: "I will make every effort to see that after my departure you will always be able to remember these things" (2 Peter 1:15). Peter died in the mid-sixties AD, so the evidence suggests that Mark wrote his Gospel either just before or just after Peter's death, in order to accurately preserve Peter's eyewitness testimony.

Was it written a long time after the events it records?

Jesus died in about AD 30. That means there was a gap of around thirty years between the events Mark records and the date he wrote about them. This is well within the lifetime of those who lived through the events he describes, so many of Mark's readers would have been able to spot any fabrications or inconsistencies. There were also many hostile eyewitnesses who were anxious to discredit him. Mark had to make sure that his account was trustworthy.

Have the original documents been accurately passed down to us?

If the originals of the Bible or any other ancient document do not exist, then the following questions need to be asked to assess the reliability of the copies:

- how old are the copies?
- how much time has elapsed between the composition of the original document and the copies that now exist?
- how many copies have been found?

➤ *The table below answers these questions for three widely trusted historical works and compares them with the New Testament. Fill in the blank space, and compare your guess with the answer at the bottom of the page.*

	Date of original document	Date of oldest surviving copy	Approximate time between original and oldest surviving copy	Number of ancient copies in existence today
THUCYDIDES' HISTORY OF THE PELOPONNESIAN WAR[2]	c. 431–400 BC	AD 900 plus a few late 1st century fragments	1,300 years	73
CAESAR'S GALLIC WAR[3]	c. 58–50 BC	AD 825	875 years	10
TACITUS' HISTORIES AND ANNALS[4]	c. AD 98–108	c. AD 850	750 years	2
THE NEW TESTAMENT[5]	AD 40–100 (Mark AD 60–65)	AD 350 (Mark 3rd century)	310 years	*

* 14,000 (approximately 5,000 Greek; 8,000 Latin; and 1,000 in other languages)

CHRISTIANITY
EPLORED

As the table shows, the interval between the original composition date of the New Testament and the date of the oldest surviving copy is comparatively small. Moreover, in contrast to the other works, there are an enormous number of early manuscript copies or portions of the New Testament.

Do other historical documents support Mark's account of Jesus?

Even without the New Testament accounts of Jesus or other Christian writings we still have plenty of evidence concerning the life and claims of Jesus. For example, the Samaritan historian Thallus (AD 52) discusses the darkness that fell during the crucifixion (recorded in Mark 15:33).[6] And Josephus, a Jewish historian writing in the first century AD, has the following to say: "Now there was about this time Jesus, a wise man, if it be lawful to call him a man; for he was a doer of wonderful works, a teacher of such men as receive the truth with pleasure. He drew over to him both many of the Jews, and many of the Gentiles. He was [the] Christ. And when Pilate, at the suggestion of the principal men among us, had condemned him to the cross, those that loved him at the first did not forsake him; for he appeared to them alive again the third day; as the divine prophets had foretold these and ten thousand other wonderful things concerning him. And the tribe of the Christians, so named from him, are not extinct at this day."[7]

EXPLORING MARK'S GOSPEL

Each week, you'll have the opportunity to explore a few chapters of Mark.

The HOME STUDY sections provide questions to help you do this. By the end of Week 6, you'll have read through the whole of Mark's Gospel.

As a group you'll also look in detail at passages of particular interest.

Here are some tips to help you get the most out of Mark's Gospel:

• Remember that Mark is writing with a clear purpose: to tell people the good news about Jesus (Mark 1:1). Mark's Gospel is not just a random collection of incidents from Jesus' life and extracts from his teaching. Instead, he carefully selects events from the life of Jesus, and deliberately places them in a certain order. He does this because he wants his readers to understand exactly who Jesus was.

A good example of this occurs in Mark 15:33–39. Why does Mark take us from events at the cross outside the city walls of Jerusalem (verses 33–37), to the temple in the heart of the city (verse 38), and then back to the cross (verse 39)? It's because he wants us to understand that these events are connected in some way and tell us something about Jesus.

- As with any book, context is very important. If you come across something you don't understand, ask yourself what has happened immediately before, and take into account what happens immediately afterwards.

- It's also important to set Mark in the context of the Bible as a whole. Just as it would make no sense to start reading Mark's Gospel at chapter 10 without thinking about what he has written in the first nine chapters, it's also vital to see how Mark fits in to the overall narrative of the Bible. Throughout the Old Testament, we read of God's gradually unfolding plan to draw people into a relationship with him. In Mark's Gospel, we see that plan reaching its conclusion. The Old Testament quotations in Mark help us to understand this.

For example, in Mark 1:2–3, Mark quotes from the Old Testament. Why does he do that? And why does he do it at this point? It's because he wants us to understand that the events he describes are part of a bigger picture.

As you explore Mark's Gospel, you will be able to discover for yourself who Jesus was, why he came, and what it would mean to follow him.

---

[1] Papias, quoted by Eusebius, *Ecclesiastical History*, Book 3, Ch. 39. Taken from *Historia Ecclesiastica: An Ecclesiastical History to the Year 324 of the Christian Era* (trans. C. F. Cruse; London: S. Bagster, 1842), p. 152.

[2] For further information on the dates and locations of the documents see P. J. Rhodes, *Thucydides History* (Warminster: Aris and Phillips, 1998), p. 30; and B. Grenfell and A. Hunt, et al., *The Oxyrhynchus Papyri* (60 vols.; London: Egypt Exploration Fund, 1898–1993). Oldest surviving copy - Florence, Biblioteca Medicea Laurenziana, LXIX.2, 10th cent.

[3] For further information on the dates and locations of the documents see L. D. Reynolds, *Texts and Transmission: A Survey of the Latin Classics* (Oxford: Clarendon Press, 1983), pp. 35–36. Oldest surviving copy - Paris, Bibliothèque Nationale, Lat. 5763, 9th cent., 2nd quarter.

[4] For further information on the dates and locations of the documents see L. D. Reynolds, *Texts and Transmission: A Survey of the Latin Classics* (Oxford: Clarendon Press, 1983), pp. 406–407. Oldest surviving copy - Florence, Biblioteca Medicea Laurenziana, 68.1, c. 850.

[5] For further information on the dates and locations of the documents see K. Aland and B. Aland, *The Text of the New Testament* (Grand Rapids: Eerdmans, 1989). Oldest surviving copy of New Testament - British Library, Add. 43725. Oldest surviving copy of Mark - Dublin, Chester Beatty Library, C.B.P. I, 3rd cent.

[6] Thallus, *History*, Book 3. Recorded by Julius Africanus in *The Extant Fragments of the Five Books of the Chronography of Julius Africanus*, XVIII (1). Taken from *The Ante-Nicene Fathers: Translations of the Writings of the Fathers down to A.D. 325*, VI (ed. Alexander Roberts and James Donaldson; rev. A. Cleveland Coxe; Grand Rapids: Eerdmans, 1979–1986), p. 136.

[7] Josephus, *The Antiquities of the Jews*, Book 18, Ch. 39 (3). Taken from *The Genuine Works of Flavius Josephus*, IV (trans. William Whiston; Edinburgh: J. and J. Fairbairn, A. Laurie, and J. Symington, 1793), p. 79.

CHRISTIANITY
E✗PLORED

INTRODUCTION

GROUP DISCUSSION 1

➤ Welcome the participants and introduce yourself. Please give each participant a Bible and a copy of the Study Guide.

➤ Ask participants to turn to Week 1 on page 11 of their Study Guide.

➤ Briefly talk through the format of their Study Guide. Explain that each week has four sections: GROUP DISCUSSION 1, TALK OUTLINE, GROUP DISCUSSION 2, and HOME STUDY. Point out that the PREFACE contains useful background information about Mark and the Bible.

➤ Show participants where to find Mark in their Bibles and explain how chapters and verses work (for example, explain what Mark 1:1 – 3:6 means, and how they would find that passage).

TALK OUTLINE

"The beginning of the gospel about Jesus Christ, the Son of God." (Mark 1:1)

• There are many reasons to suspect that God might exist: the order of the universe, the beauty of the world and the incredible design of the human body. There's also the nagging sense that nothing we do or achieve will fully satisfy us, that something is missing in life.

• But how can we know for sure that God exists? We would need him to introduce himself. And according to Mark, that's exactly what God has done. In order to introduce himself to us, he has become a man: the person we call Jesus Christ.

• Christianity is about being able to have a relationship with God. That's why "the gospel about Jesus Christ" is good news.

➤ When the following question is posed by the course leader or appears at the end of the video, encourage participants to answer it in their Study Guide and then read their answer back to the group.

➤ Note down each of their questions in the space below so that you can deal with them at some point during the course. You may also like to fill in your own answer and share it with the group.

• **If you could ask God one question, and you knew it would be answered, what would it be?**

When is God coming back.

➤ Use the questions displayed at the end of the talk to further encourage discussion. The questions are printed below and are also in the participant's Study Guide for reference.

• **What is your view of Christianity?** *TRUTH IN ACTION*

Perfect blueprint for living

• **How do you feel about making time to read Mark?**

HOME STUDY

Each week the course leader will ask participants to explore a few chapters of Mark at home. By the end of Week 6, they'll have read the whole Gospel.

➤ Read Mark 1:1 – 3:6.

Summary: Jesus' true identity begins to emerge, but the religious authorities oppose him.

Participants are asked to work through the following questions to help them understand the passage. They also have a section in which to write down any issues they'd like to discuss next time.

➤ Look through the questions and answers below ahead of time so you will be able to deal with any issues that arise next week. The ADDITIONAL NOTES FOR LEADERS on pages 67–68 will also help you to prepare. (Note: Groups are not expected to work through the HOME STUDY together.)

---

1 In Mark 1:1–13, who points to Jesus?
(look in particular at verses 2, 7 and 11)

Old Testament prophets (note that Mark's quote in vv. 2–3 refers to both Malachi 3:1 and Isaiah 40:3); John the Baptist; God the Father. *Voice of*

Isaiah 900 years before Jesus – John the Baptist God said you are my beloved son

---

2 Who is Jesus said to be in these verses?

He is the Lord whose way must be prepared; he is "more powerful" than John the Baptist who is himself a great prophet; he is God's own Son.

3 What sort of power and authority does Jesus exercise?
  (see Mark 1:16–20, 21–22, 23–28, 40–45; 2:1–12)

He exercises power and authority:

  – to call people, who immediately drop what they are doing and follow him
  – in his teaching
  – over evil spirits
  – over sickness, even the most serious illnesses
  – to forgive sins

4 What has Jesus come to do? (see Mark 1:14–15, 35–39; 2:17)

He has come to preach, to tell people to repent and believe the good news.

He has come to call sinners.

5 Notice that Jesus' priority is preaching – it comes before healing the body. Why might that be?

In his preaching, Jesus addresses an issue that is far more important than any physical infirmity: our sin.

6 Who opposes Jesus and why do you think this might be?
  (see Mark 2:6–7, 16; 3:2–6)

The religious leaders oppose him because he claims to forgive sins, because he eats with "sinners" and tax collectors, and because he heals on the Sabbath. Even here at the beginning of Jesus' ministry, the religious leaders want to kill him.

The underlying reason for their opposition is simple: everything Jesus says and does comprehensively undermines their authority. And they do not want to give up the authority that they have always enjoyed.

7 What do the opening chapters of Mark tell you about who Jesus is? What are the implications for how you relate to Jesus?

These questions are designed to help participants apply what they have learned.

Mark 1:2–3 – Mark quotes from Malachi 3:1 and Isaiah 40:3 which, in their contexts, promise a messenger who will announce the arrival of a rescuer King, the Christ, who will save God's people from judgement. The promise of a messenger is clearly fulfilled by John the Baptist in Mark 1:4–8. Even his clothing (Mark 1:6) was like that of an Old Testament prophet, in particular Elijah (2 Kings 1:8).

Evil spirits (also called "demons" in the Gospel) (Mark 1:23–27) – The Bible takes the reality of an unseen spiritual world seriously. According to the Bible, Satan is a fallen angelic being who is personal, powerful, in rebellion against God and hostile to God's people. Although Satan – and other fallen angels in alliance with him – are powerful, the New Testament shows that Jesus has overcome Satan by the power of his death on the cross (Colossians 2:15). Note: if this topic arises, deal with it briefly but don't allow it to dominate the session.

Pharisees – This group did not just obey the Old Testament Scriptures but adhered to a stricter tradition, so they were seen as some of the most holy men in Israel. They viewed anyone who did not observe the same rigorous rules as a "sinner" and an outcast (see Mark 2:15–16). Jesus called them "hypocrites," which literally means "play-actors," because of their public displays of religion and self-righteousness. He strongly condemns them in passages such as Mark 7:6–9 and Matthew 23.

"Bridegroom" (Mark 2:19) – Jesus is making the point that all fasting is totally inappropriate in his presence, just as it would be for wedding guests to mourn at a wedding. Jesus is identifying himself as the bridegroom of God's people, promised by the Old Testament (Isaiah 54:5; 62:4–5; Hosea 2:16–20). Because Jesus came to deal with our sin, we should be celebrating, not mourning.

"Sabbath" (Mark 2:23) – Sabbath means "cease" or "rest" and is derived from the Hebrew word used in Genesis 2:2 where God "ceased" or "rested" from his work of creation. It is therefore linked to the biblical concept of "rest" whereby God's people dwell in God's place under God's gracious rule (Genesis 1–2). While this state of rest was lost at the Fall (Genesis 3), God promised to restore it to his people (Genesis 12:1–3; 17:8). The Sabbath was an opportunity for God's people to remember God's creation and how he rescued them from Egypt (see Exodus 20:8–11; Deuteronomy 5:12–15).

The disciples eat corn (Mark 2:23–26) – The Pharisees accused Jesus' followers of law-breaking: namely, "reaping" on the Sabbath (Exodus 34:21). What the disciples are doing can hardly be construed as "reaping." But instead of pointing that out, Jesus refers to David's act in 1 Samuel 21:1–6. He observes that David is not condemned by Scripture for doing what he did, and so Jesus draws attention to the Pharisees' narrow (and unscriptural) interpretation of the law.

"Herodians" (Mark 3:6) – These were loyal supporters of Herod Antipas, the puppet King of Judea, who depended on the controlling Roman Empire for his power. They would have seen Jesus as a threat to Herod's rule.

CHRISTIANITY
E⁇PLORED

GROUP DISCUSSION 1

➤ Ask participants to turn to Week 2 on page 15 of their Study Guide.

➤ Ask if anyone has any questions arising from last week's HOME STUDY, and discuss as necessary.

➤ Ask participants to turn to Mark 2:1–12. One of the leaders should read the passage aloud and then the group should work through the study below. The answers are printed here for your reference. The ADDITIONAL NOTES FOR LEADERS on page 70 may also help you. (Note: participants should not be asked to read aloud during the course).

---

1 The passage opens by telling us that so many people had gathered to hear Jesus that there was no room left. Why had so many people come to hear Jesus? (look at Mark 1:27–28, 32–34, 45 for clues)

Jesus' teaching and healing have amazed people, and news about him was spreading.

2 Why did these people bring their friend to Jesus?

To have him healed of his paralysis.

3 In view of the situation, what is surprising about what Jesus says in Mark 2:5?

Jesus says "Son, your sins are forgiven." The man was lowered through the roof to be healed, not to have his sins forgiven.

---

4 Why were the teachers of the law so annoyed about Jesus' remark? (see Mark 2:6–7)

Jesus is claiming to do that which only God can do, something the teachers of the law see clearly (Mark 2:7). So they conclude that he is blaspheming.

5 Were they right?

Yes and no. Yes, only God can forgive sin. No, Jesus isn't blaspheming because he is God. *take mad - lied or god.*

6 How do we know that Jesus has authority to forgive sin? (see Mark 2:8–12)

He healed the man. *you cannot see and forgiven but Jesus healed man as proof*

7 What does this incident imply about who Jesus is? (see Mark 2:7)

He is God. ("Who can forgive sins but God alone?")

8 Why do you think Jesus said, "Son, your sins are forgiven" before healing the man?

The man's greatest need is to have his sins forgiven, not to be healed. Note: This is because – as we shall see next week – sin is much more deadly than any physical disability. *As a teaching method -*

ADDITIONAL NOTES FOR LEADERS

"Son, your sins are forgiven" (Mark 2:5) – Jesus is not implying that there is a direct correlation between the man's sin and his disability (see what Jesus says about the tower in Siloam in Luke 13:1–5).

Blasphemy (Mark 2:7) – Only God can forgive sin because God is the one against whom we rebel. So when Jesus claims to forgive sin, he is putting himself in God's place. The religious authorities see this as blasphemy – a slander against God. Either Jesus is a blasphemer or, if Jesus is God, then the teachers of the law are the ones guilty of blasphemy!

"Son of Man" (Mark 2:10) – Jesus frequently refers to himself in this way. It recalls Daniel 7:9–14, in which the "son of man" was the name of the one who approached the Ancient of Days (God), and was given authority to rule over everyone forever, starting from the final judgement.

CHRISTIANITY
EXPLORED

"Who is this? Even the wind and the waves obey him!" (Mark 4:41)

- It's important to get Jesus' identity right – otherwise we'll relate to him in the wrong way.

- Mark presents us with five blocks of evidence, five different areas in which Jesus demonstrated the power and authority of God.

- Jesus demonstrated power and authority:
  - to teach (Mark 1:21–22)
  - over sickness (Mark 1:29–31)
  - over nature (Mark 4:35–41)
  - over death (Mark 5:35–42)
  - to forgive sins (Mark 2:1–12)

GROUP DISCUSSION 2

➤ *Use the questions displayed at the end of the talk to encourage discussion. The questions are printed below and are also in the participant's* Study Guide *for reference.*

- **What is your view of Jesus?**

- **What do you think of the five blocks of evidence Mark gives us?**

Sin is living without Reference to God.

➤ *You may find it useful to ask your group to consider the following: "A man who was merely a man and said the sort of things Jesus said would not be a great moral teacher... Either this man was, and is, the Son of God: or else a madman or something worse."*[1]

---

[1] C. S. Lewis, *Mere Christianity* (London: Fount, 1997), p. 43.

22nd APRIL.

✗

➤ *Read Mark 3:7 – 5:43.*

Summary: Jesus' identity continues to emerge as he teaches and displays miraculous power.

Participants are asked to work through the following questions to help them understand the passage. They also have a section in which to write down any issues they'd like to discuss next time.

➤ *Look through the questions and answers below ahead of time so you will be able to deal with any issues that arise next week. The ADDITIONAL NOTES FOR LEADERS on page 74 will also help you to prepare.*

**1 What does Jesus exercise power and authority over?
(see Mark 4:35–41; 5:1–20, 25–34, 35–43)**

He exercises power and authority:

– over nature, even at its most violent

– over powerful evil spirits

– over the most serious illness

– over death

2 What does this add to what we saw of Jesus' power and authority in Mark 1:1 – 3:6?

We see Jesus exercise power and authority in ways we have not seen before – for example, over nature and death.

3 What is the disciples' concern in Mark 4:38? What is Jesus' assessment of them in Mark 4:40?

They are afraid they are going to drown.

Jesus says they are afraid because they have no faith.

Jesus does not appear to care.

CHRISTIANITY
EXPLORED

4 Describe the situation of the woman in Mark 5:25–26. What happens to her in Mark 5:27–29? What is Jesus' assessment of her in Mark 5:34?

Her condition is desperate – she has had this disease for twelve years.

She is healed when she touches Jesus' cloak.

Her faith has healed her.

5 Describe the situation of Jairus in Mark 5:35. What is Jesus' assessment of him in Mark 5:36?

His daughter is dead. The situation is hopeless – "Why bother the teacher any more?"

Jesus tells him not to be afraid but to believe (in other words, to have faith).

6 What do these incidents teach us about who Jesus is?

He has absolutely no difficulty in dealing with the most extreme, most hopeless situations.

7 What are the different ways in which people respond to Jesus? (see Mark 4:40–41; 5:15, 34, 36)

In all cases it is either faith or fear.

The disciples are afraid.

The crowd who see him heal a demon-possessed man are afraid.

The woman has faith.

Jairus has faith.

8 Which of these responses to Jesus do you most relate to?

This question is designed to help participants apply what they have learned.

"Judea, Jerusalem, Idumea..." (Mark 3:8) – The places mentioned refer to the boundaries of the land originally allotted to Judah (Joshua 15). By Jesus' day much of this land was inhabited by Gentiles (non-Jews).

The appointing of twelve apostles (Mark 3:13–19) – Significantly, Jesus calls the twelve apostles on a mountainside. In the Old Testament God revealed himself to his people on mountains (cf. Genesis 8; Exodus 19; and 1 Kings 18) and there were twelve tribes of Israel (Genesis 49).

"He is possessed by Beelzebub" (Mark 3:22) – Beelzebub is another name for the devil. Note that the religious authorities did not question whether Jesus was powerful or whether the miracles had happened, they simply question the source of his power. They claim that Jesus is possessed by the devil and is driving out demons. Jesus replies that their claim is ludicrous – after all, if the "prince of demons" really was driving out other demons, then his actions would be self-defeating.

"whoever blasphemes against the Holy Spirit will never be forgiven" (Mark 3:29) – Jesus warns the religious leaders that attributing his authority to evil (Mark 3:22, 30) is blasphemy because his authority comes from God. Jesus is the Son of Man with the authority to forgive sin (Mark 2:10), and to reject him is to reject forgiveness. Such rejection is blasphemy, or slander, against the work of God's Spirit through Jesus. Jesus' warning has nothing to do with swearing at the Holy Spirit – in simple terms, it means rejecting the only way of forgiveness that God has provided. Of course, this sin is only unforgivable for as long as a person goes on committing it. Many of the religious leaders repented later, and so were forgiven (Acts 6:7).

"parables" (Mark 4:2) – Jesus used this method of teaching to convey spiritual truths. Parables have a clear surface meaning (often just one main point), but also a deeper meaning, which Jesus explains to those who listen (Mark 4:1–34). There is a spiritual principle here: "to everyone who has, more will be given" (Luke 19:26). The disciples were spiritually intrigued by the parables and drew nearer to Jesus to hear the explanation. However, to the unconcerned, the parables remained merely curious stories. They hear, but do not understand (Mark 4:12).

"otherwise they might turn and be forgiven" (Mark 4:12) – The quote comes from Isaiah 6:9–10. From the context of that passage, it is clear that Israel had already shut her eyes and ears against God. Verses 9–10 therefore describe God's judgement on stubborn hearts. The quote can equally be applied to some of those listening to the parables Jesus tells.

CHRISTIANITY
E✝PLORED

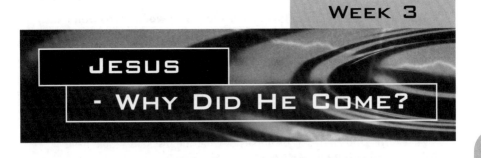

JESUS
- WHY DID HE COME?

GROUP DISCUSSION 1

➤ Ask participants to turn to Week 3 on page 21 of their Study Guide.

➤ Ask if anyone has any questions arising from last week's HOME STUDY, and discuss as necessary.

➤ Ask participants to turn to Mark 4:35–41. One of the leaders should read the passage aloud and then the group should work through the study below. The answers are printed here for your reference. The ADDITIONAL NOTES FOR LEADERS on page 76 may also help you.

1 Why are the disciples afraid in Mark 4:37–38?

They think they are going to die. Remember, some of the disciples are experienced fishermen; they're not easily frightened.

2 What is so remarkable about the way in which Jesus calms the storm? (see Mark 4:39)

He did it with a few simple words. The fact that Jesus instantly calmed not just the furious wind, but the huge waves as well – even though waves normally persist for hours or even days after the wind dies down – shows that a miracle has taken place.

3 What is surprising about Jesus' response to the disciples? (see Mark 4:40)

He rebukes them for being frightened of losing their lives. He tells them they should have faith.

4 Why don't the disciples have faith – in other words, why don't they trust Jesus? (see Mark 4:41)

They don't know who he is.

5 What should the disciples have understood from this incident, bearing in mind they were Jews who would have been steeped in the Old Testament? (one of the leaders should read aloud the following verses from the Psalms as examples of what the disciples would have known – Psalms 89:9; 65:5–7; 107:23–30)

The Old Testament makes it clear that only God has power and authority over the wind and waves. The disciples should have seen that Jesus is God.

6 How would *you* answer the disciples' question in Mark 4:41 – "Who is this? Even the wind and the waves obey him!"

This question is designed to reveal whether the participants have grasped who Jesus is. Rather than pressing them for an answer, it may be more appropriate to ask participants to reflect on this in their own time.

ADDITIONAL NOTES FOR LEADERS

"Do you still have no faith?" (Mark 4:40) – Despite all the evidence they've witnessed, the disciples still don't have faith in Jesus (note: to "have faith" in someone means to trust him or her). The disciples express terror rather than trust both before *and* after Jesus acts. Interestingly, just before this miracle, Jesus has told three parables making the point that God's word is powerful. He then calms the storm with a word. The disciples should have drawn the obvious conclusion.

CHRISTIANITY
E/PLORED

"I have not come to call the righteous, but sinners." (Mark 2:17)

• The reason that the world is not as it should be is because we are not as we should be.

• When asked what the greatest commandment was, Jesus replied, "Love the Lord your God with all your heart and with all your soul and with all your mind and with all your strength" (Mark 12:30). But none of us have lived like that.

• We've all rebelled against God, and the Bible calls this "sin."

• Jesus tells us that "sin" comes "from within," from our "hearts" (Mark 7:20–22).

• This means that we're all in danger, whether we realize it or not (Mark 9:43–47).

• Jesus came to rescue us from our sin.

WEEK 3

GROUP DISCUSSION 2

➤ *Use the questions displayed at the end of the talk to encourage discussion. The questions are printed below and are also in the participant's* Study Guide *for reference.*

• **Do you agree that you're in danger?**

yes but no if we are christians

• **How would you feel if your every thought, word and action was displayed on the walls for everyone to see?**

not good

• **What's your reaction to Jesus' words in Mark chapter 9, verses 43–47?**

➤ Read Mark 6:1 – 8:29.

Summary: Despite the amazement that Jesus continues to generate, many reject him. Jesus explains why.

Participants are asked to work through the following questions to help them understand the passage. They also have a section in which to write down any issues they'd like to discuss next time.

➤ *Look through the questions and answers below ahead of time so you will be able to deal with any issues that arise next week. The ADDITIONAL NOTES FOR LEADERS on pages 79–80 will also help you to prepare.*

---

1 What does this passage add to what we've seen of Jesus' power and authority in chapters 1–5?
(see Mark 6:32–44, 47–48; 7:31–37; 8:1–10, 22–26)

He is able to feed vast crowds of people from a handful of provisions.

He is able to heal the blind and deaf and mute.

He is able to walk on water.

The passages here are full of Old Testament imagery, pointing to the fact that Jesus is the rescuer promised in the Old Testament. See ADDITIONAL NOTES on Mark 6:34 on page 80.

2 How are people responding to Jesus as they see his power and authority? (see Mark 6:1–6, 14–16, 51–56; 7:37; 8:11)

Many are utterly amazed at what he is doing and are speculating wildly about who he is, but no-one seems to be anywhere near the right answer.

Others, however, are suspicious and offended by what they see.

3 According to Jesus, what is the real need of the people? (see Mark 6:34; 7:14–23)

They (and we) are like sheep without a shepherd, lost and in need.

They (and we) have hearts out of which spring all kinds of evil – this means that at the deepest, most unalterable level they (and we) are "unclean." In other words, we are unacceptable to God.

Fellowship with God is broken by sin · not unclean food etc

---

4 In view of all that Jesus has said and done, what is so surprising about the disciples' response? (see Mark 6:35–37, 51; 7:17–18; 8:4, 14–21)

They still don't understand who Jesus is, what he can do or what he is saying.

5 Now that you're halfway through Mark's Gospel, and have read about the amazing things that Jesus said and did, how would you answer Jesus' question in Mark 8:29?

This question is designed to help participants apply what they have learned.

ADDITIONAL NOTES FOR LEADERS

Jesus' brothers and sisters (Mark 6:3) – These were the natural children of Joseph and Mary, conceived after the birth of Jesus. See also Mark 3:32. This helps to answer the question as to whether Mary remained a virgin after the birth of Jesus. In addition, Matthew 1:25 certainly implies that Joseph and Mary had a normal sexual relationship after Jesus' birth.

Jesus sends out the Twelve (Mark 6:7–11) – Jesus sends out the twelve apostles, telling them to expect some to accept and some to reject the gospel (Mark 6:10–11). They are to reject those who, by refusing to listen, reject them. The reference to shaking off dust refers to an act by Jews on returning to Israel from Gentile countries, which they viewed as "unclean." For the disciples to do it in a Jewish village was akin to calling the village Gentile! It is a mark of judgement (see also Acts 13:51).

John the Baptist (Mark 6:14–29) – Mark inserts this account of the death of John the Baptist into the account of the ministry of the Twelve to make an important point (Mark 6:7–13, 30). It answers the implied question of Mark 6:1–13: why don't people see who Jesus is? People reject Jesus because, like Herod, they will not repent. In other words, they will not turn from their rebellion against God.

"like sheep without a shepherd" (Mark 6:34) – In Ezekiel 34, Israel is described as being like sheep without a shepherd because her leaders had not done their job properly (Ezekiel 34:1–6). As a result, God promised to come himself to rescue his people (Ezekiel 34:16). Jesus is that rescuer, acting as God's shepherd by feeding the sheep in a miraculous way (Mark 6:30–44; 8:1–10), as God himself had done when rescuing Israel from Egypt (Exodus 16:32–35). Further evidence that Jesus is indeed God is provided by the fact that Jesus is also said to "pass by" the disciples as he walks on water, in language reminiscent of God passing by Moses at the time he received the stone tablets (Mark 6:48; cf. Exodus 34:1–9).

Syro-Phoenician woman (Mark 7:24–30) – Mark records this incident in order to show that the rescue Jesus brings also applies to Gentiles. The woman was not a Jew but a Gentile from near the city of Tyre. The children in the analogy refer to the Jews, while "dogs" was a common term used to describe Gentiles. She sees that while the Jews are rescued first, the Gentiles will also be included. It should, therefore, come as no surprise to see Jesus performing a feeding miracle in a Gentile area (Mark 8:1–10).

The deaf and mute man (Mark 7:31–37) – You will recall that, in Mark 4:11–12, Mark quoted Isaiah 6:9–10, where Israel is described as blind and deaf. However, God promised that when he rescued his people he would open blind eyes, unstop deaf ears and enable mute tongues to speak (Isaiah 35:5–6). Not only does Jesus heal a deaf and mute man, he also heals a blind man (Mark 8:22–25).

Why did Jesus tell healed people not to tell anyone? (Mark 7:36) – While Christ's healings were a necessary part of demonstrating his power and authority, Jesus did not want to become a sideshow, with people following him just to see signs and wonders. He rejected such people (Mark 8:11–13; John 4:48). If people would not respond to the preaching of the kingdom of God, which called for repentance and faith (Mark 1:15), miracles alone would not convince them. He had not come to perform miracles to satisfy people's curiosity, but to die for them. Moreover, the desire for miracles hampered his ministry (see Mark 1:35–38, 45).

"the yeast of the Pharisees and that of Herod" (Mark 8:15) – "Yeast" is generally used in the New Testament to refer to the corrupting influence of someone or something. Just as a tiny amount of yeast has a great effect on the whole batch of dough, so Jesus warns against being affected by the sinful attitudes of the Pharisees and Herod.

JESUS

- HIS DEATH

GROUP DISCUSSION 1

➢ Ask participants to turn to Week 4 on page 27 of their Study Guide.

➢ Ask if anyone has any questions arising from last week's HOME STUDY, and discuss as necessary.

➢ Ask participants to turn to Mark 8:17–29. One of the leaders should read the passage aloud and then the group should work through the study below. The answers are printed here for your reference. The ADDITIONAL NOTES FOR LEADERS on page 82 may also help you.

---

1 Generally speaking, who do people today believe Jesus to be? On what do they base their views?

Answers are likely to include a good man, a wise teacher, a prophet etc. These views can be based on hearsay, the media, Sunday school, religious education lessons etc.

2 How does Jesus describe the disciples in Mark 8:17, 18 and 21?

They do not see or understand. Their hearts are hardened. They have eyes but fail to see and ears but fail to hear.

---

3 "Do you still not understand?" What should the disciples have understood? (see Mark 8:17–21; see also Exodus 16:11–15, where God miraculously feeds people in the desert)

Twice Jesus had fed large crowds of people in a remote place where no food was available. As Jews, they should have remembered the way God fed the children of Israel by giving them the manna in the desert. The disciples should have understood that Jesus is God – or at least that he is doing God-like things.

4 What happens in Mark 8:29, and why is this important?

Peter sees that Jesus is the Christ. His moment of recognition is important – indeed it is a turning point in Mark – because none of the twelve disciples have so far understood this, despite all that Jesus has said and done.

5 Why do you think Mark describes a miracle (the healing of the blind man) between Mark 8:21 and Mark 8:29? How have the disciples come to understand who Jesus is?

In Mark 8:21 the disciples do not see or understand who Jesus is, but in Mark 8:29 they have finally grasped his identity. The disciples have come to see who Jesus is by means of a miracle, just as the blind man saw by means of a miracle.

6 In Mark 8:29, Jesus asks: "But what about you? Who do you say I am?" How would you answer and why?

This question is designed to reveal where the participants stand with Christ. Rather than pressing them for an answer, it may be more appropriate for participants to reflect on this in their own time.

ADDITIONAL NOTES FOR LEADERS

The two-part healing (Mark 8:22–25) – Mark is seeking to prepare us for Peter's "partial" sight. When Peter announces that Jesus is the Christ in Mark 8:29 he is like the man in Mark 8:24 (he has partial sight). It is clear from the verses that follow – where Peter rebukes Jesus – that although he has understood who Jesus is, he has not yet realized why Jesus has come (Mark 8:30–33).

CHRISTIANITY
E*X*PLORED

"For even the Son of Man did not come to be served, but to serve, and to give his life as a ransom for many." (Mark 10:45)

• Jesus went to his death willingly and quite deliberately. In fact, he knew it was necessary.

• As Jesus died on the cross, the darkness that fell was a sign of God's anger and judgement. And Jesus' cry – "My God, my God, why have you forsaken me?" (Mark 15:34) – shows that Jesus was abandoned by God.

• He was abandoned so that we need never be. He died taking the anger and judgement that our sin deserves. God was sacrificing himself by sending his Son to die in our place.

• As Jesus died, the curtain in the temple was torn in two from top to bottom. This illustrates the fact that Jesus' death opens the way for sinful people to come into God's presence.

• Mark records the reactions of those who witness Jesus' death:
> – the busy soldiers (Mark 15:24)
> – the self-satisfied religious leaders (Mark 15:31–32)
> – the cowardly Pontius Pilate (Mark 15:15)
> – the detached bystander (Mark 15:35–36)
> – the Roman centurion, who recognized that Jesus was "the Son of God" (Mark 15:39)

WEEK 4

GROUP DISCUSSION 2

➤ *Use the questions displayed at the end of the talk to encourage discussion. The questions are printed below and are also in the participant's Study Guide for reference.*

• Can you identify with any of the reactions to Jesus' death on the cross?

• Jesus said he came "to give his life as a ransom for many" (Mark 10:45). How do you feel about that?

➤ Read Mark 8:30 – 10:52.

Summary: Jesus predicts his own death in detail, and teaches his followers what it will mean for them.

Participants are asked to work through the following questions to help them understand the passage. They also have a section in which to write down any issues they'd like to discuss next time.

➤ Look through the questions and answers below ahead of time so you will be able to deal with any issues that arise next week. The ADDITIONAL NOTES FOR LEADERS on pages 85–86 will also help you to prepare.

[handwritten: on Pentecost ; or Resurrection. ✓ ① What does it mean? Does it mean they will see him rise after death? or the transforming...]

1 Jesus predicts his own death three times. What does he say "must" and "will" happen? (see Mark 8:31, 9:31 and 10:33–34. Note that "Son of Man" is Jesus' way of referring to himself.)

He must suffer, be rejected by the religious leaders, be killed and, three days later, rise again.

He will be betrayed.

He will be handed over to the Gentiles (that is, the Romans) by the religious leaders in Jerusalem.

He will be mocked, spat on, flogged and killed.

2 Why must Jesus die? (see Mark 10:45)

Jesus must suffer and die as a ransom for many.

3 Three times Jesus predicts his own death and Mark records the disciples' response each time. How do the disciples respond and why? (see Mark 8:32–33; 9:33–35; 10:35–45)

Each time Jesus tells his disciples about his death, an incident immediately follows that shows that the disciples have not understood his teaching:

– Peter rebukes Jesus because he hasn't understood that Jesus must suffer and die – he has in mind the things of men, not God.

– the disciples argue about who is the greatest, because they haven't understood Jesus' teaching on serving others.

– James and John want to sit next to Jesus in his glory, because – again – they haven't learned to put others first.

CHRISTIANITY
EXPLORED

4 What has Jesus taught the disciples that following him will mean? (see Mark 8:34)

They must deny themselves, take up their cross and follow him.

5 Peter sees that Jesus is the Christ (that is, God's anointed King), but he doesn't yet behave as if that were true (see Mark 8:32). How should he have behaved? How should you behave towards Jesus?

Clearly, it is inappropriate to rebuke a king, not least God's anointed King. Peter should by now have learned to trust Jesus. He should have denied his own preconceived ideas about what it means to follow Jesus.

The second part of this question is designed to help participants reflect on their own attitudes to Jesus.

ADDITIONAL NOTES FOR LEADERS

"Get behind me, Satan!" (Mark 8:32–33) – Peter had recognized that Jesus was the Christ, but he could not understand why Jesus had to suffer and die. Jesus recognizes in Peter's words a temptation to reject God's plan that the Christ should endure the cross.

"will not taste death before they see the kingdom of God come with power" (Mark 9:1) – This refers to the transfiguration of Jesus, which is recorded immediately after this (Mark 9:2–7).

"Elijah and Moses" (Mark 9:4) – Both of these people represent the Old Testament: Moses represents the law and Elijah represents the prophets. The fact that they talk with Jesus demonstrates that he is the one to whom the Old Testament bears witness.

"Elijah does come first" (Mark 9:11–13) – The disciples have failed to recognize that John the Baptist was the Elijah-like messenger promised in Malachi 4:5–6 who would be the forerunner of "the Lord." Elijah was a prophet in the eighth century BC, who lived out in the wilderness, wearing animal skins and a leather belt (2 Kings 1:8). This is how John the Baptist is described in Mark 1:6. Jesus makes it clear that John was the fulfillment of the prophecy concerning Elijah.

"If your hand causes you to sin, cut it off..." etc. (Mark 9:43–48) – Jesus obviously did not intend that a Christian should physically cut off a hand or foot, or pluck out an eye. Jesus is using hyperbole to make a point: "If anything is stopping you from entering the kingdom of God, it is better to take drastic action to rid yourself of that impediment, whatever it is, than end up in hell forever." Indeed, it must be remembered that according to Jesus our problem is not our hands, or feet or eyes – but our hearts (Mark 7:18–23). We cannot cut out our hearts without dying, of course, so we are powerless to help ourselves. We need the rescue that only Jesus can provide.

Divorce (Mark 10:1–12) – Jesus is making it clear that divorce is always against the perfect purpose of God. God's plan, since creation, is that married people should live together for their whole lives (Mark 10:6–9; cf. Genesis 2:24). Jesus also emphasized that if people seek a divorce because they have found an alternative partner, such action is adultery (Mark 10:11–12). It is only because people's hearts are so hard (Mark 10:5) that divorce could ever be permitted. The two-fold danger is either that we use the concession of verse 5 as an excuse for deliberate sin, or, alternatively, that we think of divorce as cutting us forever out of the will of God. Christ came to die for all sin, including the failures of divorce. In talking to the Samaritan woman in John 4, Jesus knew that she had already been divorced five times and was now living with a sixth man. But even knowing these facts, he still freely offered her acceptance and forgiveness: "If you knew the gift of God and who it is that asks you for a drink, you would have asked him and he would have given you living water" (John 4:10).

"receive the kingdom of God like a little child" (Mark 10:15) – Jesus is calling on the disciples to realize that they have nothing to offer and must therefore depend fully on God, just as a little child depends fully on its parents. Jesus' phrase here does not imply innocence or purity – neither of which are traits of most children!

"Can you drink the cup I drink..." (Mark 10:38) – In the Old Testament, "the cup" was generally a reference to suffering. It also referred to the cup of God's wrath (see Jeremiah 25:15–16). In verse 38, Jesus is showing that the disciples don't know what they are talking about. They, unlike Jesus, have their own sin to deal with and therefore cannot suffer God's wrath on other people's behalf; a sinless substitute is required. However, Jesus adds – in verse 39 – that they will suffer.

CHRISTIANITY
EXPLORED

WHAT IS

GRACE?

GROUP DISCUSSION 1

➤ Ask *participants to turn to Week 5 on page 33 of their* Study Guide.

➤ *Ask if anyone has any questions arising from last week's HOME STUDY, and discuss as necessary.*

➤ *Ask participants to turn to Mark 10:17–22. One of the leaders should read the passage aloud and then the group should work through the study below. The answers are printed here for your reference. The ADDITIONAL NOTES FOR LEADERS on page 88 may also help you.*

---

1 What do we learn about the man and his attitude to Jesus in Mark 10:17?

He is eager to speak with Jesus – he runs up to him. He is humble and respects Jesus – he falls on his knees before him and calls him "Good teacher." He is concerned about his eternal destiny – he wants to know what he can do to inherit eternal life.

2 What should the man have understood about himself from what Jesus says in Mark 10:18? And how should he have reacted?

If "no-one is good – except God alone" then the man should have understood that he is not "good." With that in mind, he should have seen his desperate need for God's mercy. (Jesus' words also imply that if Jesus is indeed "good," then he must be God.)

---

3 What did Jesus expect the man to notice about his list of the commandments in Mark 10:19? (compare what Jesus says with the list of commandments in Deuteronomy 5:6–21)

The man should have noticed that the first four commandments are missing.

4 So, what should the man have understood about himself from what Jesus says in Mark 10:19? Again, how should he have reacted?

Jesus is deliberately drawing his attention to the commandments concerning the way we should treat God: have no other gods, have no idols, do not misuse God's name, keep his Sabbath. Jesus' words are therefore intended to show the man that, despite his claim, he has not kept the commandments – he wants him to understand that it's impossible for anyone to do so.

Again, the man should have reacted by seeing his desperate need for God's mercy.

5 How does Jesus expose the man's failure to keep the first commandment? (see Deuteronomy 5:7 and Mark 10:21–22)

Jesus asks the man to give away his wealth and follow him. The man will not do so. Clearly, his wealth comes first, before God.

6 Where does the man place his confidence – with wealth or with God? Where do you place your confidence?

This question is designed to help participants apply what they have learned.

ADDITIONAL NOTES FOR LEADERS

"what must I do to inherit eternal life?" (Mark 10:17) – The problem with the man's question is that he believes he can contribute something to his salvation. He cannot, because – like all of us – he is sinful. The only means of salvation God has provided is the sacrificial death of his Son on the cross.

He is no fool who gives what he cannot keep to get what he cannot lose.

CHRISTIANITY
E✝PLORED

"For it is by grace you have been saved, through faith – and this not from yourselves, it is the gift of God – not by works, so that no-one can boast." (Ephesians 2:8–9)

- We can't make ourselves acceptable to God by doing "good things." These things may be wonderful in themselves, but they can't solve the problem of our sin.

- We are only acceptable to God because of Jesus' death. When we look at what happened at the cross, we see God freely offering us forgiveness.

- This is something we cannot earn and do not deserve. And that's grace: God behaving toward us in a way we simply do not deserve.

- We don't have to pretend to be something we're not. We don't have to be constantly proving ourselves to God. God's love for us is unconditional.

GROUP DISCUSSION 2

➤ *Use the questions displayed at the end of the talk to encourage discussion. The questions are printed below and are also in the participant's* Study Guide *for reference.*

- **If you were in the bishop's place, would you have given Valjean the candlesticks as well?**

- **Has grace made a difference to your view of God?**

- **What do people generally do to be accepted by God, if they bother at all?**

➤ *Read Mark 11:1 – 13:37.*

Summary: Jesus goes to Jerusalem, and comes into confrontation with the religious authorities.

Participants are asked to work through the following questions to help them understand the passage. They also have a section in which to write down any issues they'd like to discuss next time.

➤ *Look through the questions and answers below ahead of time so you will be able to deal with any issues that arise next week. The ADDITIONAL NOTES FOR LEADERS on page 92 will also help you to prepare.*

---

1 What is the crowd's attitude towards Jesus as he arrives in Jerusalem? (see Mark 11:8–10)

They are respectful, joyful and expectant – some spread their cloaks on the road, others spread branches. They welcome him with shouts of praise. (Note: "Hosanna" is a Hebrew word meaning "Save us!")

2 What is the religious authorities' attitude to Jesus in Mark 11:18 and Mark 12:12?

They fear him because of his popularity with the crowd. They look for an opportunity to arrest Jesus and kill him.

3 As a result of this attitude, how do they treat Jesus? (see Mark 11:27–33; 12:13–17, 18–27)

They question Jesus' authority.

They're two-faced: they flatter him, but seek to trap him with trick questions.

Their questions are not genuine – they just want Jesus to confirm what they already think.

CHRISTIANITY
E⳽PLORED

4 The religious authorities are steeped in the Old Testament and Jesus knows how familiar they are with it (in Mark 11:17 he says, "Is it not written..." and in Mark 12:10, "Haven't you read this scripture..."). What is the significance of the detail in Mark 11:1–10? (see Zechariah 9:9) What should the religious authorities have understood?

They should have understood that Jesus is the King promised in Zechariah and throughout the Old Testament. Jesus is the fulfillment of Old Testament prophecy.

5 Why, then, do they reject Jesus? (see Mark 12:24, 38–40)

They haven't understood Scripture or God's power because they are proud, conceited, hypocritical people, more concerned with outward appearance than anything else.

6 How will you treat Jesus if "you do not know the Scriptures or the power of God?"

This question is designed to help participants apply what they have learned.

ch 13.

V. 30 : I tell you the truth, this generation will certainly not pass away until all these things have happened.

Jesus curses the fig-tree (Mark 11:12–14, 20–21) – Mark interweaves the cursing of the fig-tree with the events in the temple (Mark 11:15–19, 27–33). In the same way that Jesus curses the fig-tree for fruitlessness, he condemns Israel's religion – symbolized by the temple – as fruitless.

One bride for seven brothers? (Mark 12:18–27) – In Jesus' day there were two major religious groups: the Pharisees, who believed in life after death, and the Sadducees, who said that death was the end. They had no hope of life beyond the grave, or of resurrection (Mark 12:18). So the Sadducees came up with this question to trick Jesus (Mark 12:18–23). In his answer to them, in Mark 12:24–27, Jesus says two things. First, Jesus tells them that there is life beyond the grave but there are no married relationships in heaven. Secondly, he makes it clear that because God is the God of the living, and is referred to as "the God of Abraham, Isaac and Jacob" it must mean that Abraham, Isaac and Jacob are yet living.

"The abomination that causes desolation" (Mark 13:14) – The parallel passage in Luke describes "Jerusalem surrounded by her armies," so the phrase refers to the occasion in AD 65 when Roman armies surrounded Jerusalem after a political uprising. After a horrific five-year conflict, the Roman armies entered the city, desecrated the Holy of Holies in the temple, then proceeded to pull down the temple and destroy the city. Jesus' words in Mark 13 therefore came to pass.

CHRISTIANITY
E✝PLORED

WEEK 6

JESUS

- HIS RESURRECTION

GROUP DISCUSSION 1

➢ Ask participants to turn to Week 6 on page 39 of their Study Guide.

➢ Ask if anyone has any questions arising from last week's HOME STUDY, and discuss as necessary.

➢ Ask participants to turn to Mark 12:1–11. One of the leaders should read the passage aloud and then the group should work through the study below. The answers are printed here for your reference. The ADDITIONAL NOTES FOR LEADERS on page 95 may also help you.

---

1 Who is the "man" in Mark 12:1 and·"the owner" in Mark 12:9?

God.   *Tenants are Jews. Jesus is the*
son.   Israel.
we are the tenant either good or bad.

2 What do we learn about God from Mark 12:1–2?

God is generous – the vineyard he sets up is well-equipped and well-planned.

God entrusts people with good things – he rents the vineyard out to tenants.

He made a covenant with them.

3 How do the tenants treat the owner in Mark 12:3–5?

They do not give him what is due to him – the fruit of the harvest.

They also mistreat all his representatives.

---

4 What do we learn about God from Mark 12:3–5?

He is patient and merciful. Even though the tenants ignore him and treat his representatives violently, he persistently offers them the chance to do the right thing.

5 What does the owner do in Mark 12:6? Who does this remind you of?

He sends his son, whom he loves. This is the way God describes Jesus at his baptism and transfiguration.

6 How do the tenants treat the son? (see Mark 12:7–8)

They know exactly who he is (v. 7 "This is the heir"), but they kill him anyway.

7 What do they expect the outcome of their actions will be? (see Mark 12:7–8)

They expect to get the vineyard for themselves, without ever having to give the owner what is due to him. They do not expect to be condemned for their wrongdoing.

8 What is the owner's response? (see Mark 12:9)

Ultimately, he will reject those who have persistently rejected him. Justice will be done.

9 Do you think the tenants would have behaved as they did if they believed that the owner would judge them?

This question is designed to help participants reflect on their own view of judgement.

10 In Mark 12:10–11, Jesus quotes Psalm 118, applying the quote to himself. What is "marvellous" about Jesus being rejected?

God makes the rejection of his own Son the means of rescue for rebellious people.

CHRISTIANITY
E⊀PLORED

Vineyard – The vineyard was a common Old Testament symbol of Israel. In particular, this passage is very similar to Isaiah 5, where the people of Israel are rebuked for the terrible way they have rejected God and are told that God's righteous judgement will come. Jesus' hearers would have understood that the "man" in the parable was God, that the "vineyard" was the people of God, and that the missing fruit was allegiance to the Son.

Capstone – This is the most important stone; the foundation stone.

TALK OUTLINE

"He has risen! ... just as he told you." (Mark 16:6–7)

• Three days after Jesus' death and burial, Mark records how the women who had watched Jesus die go to the tomb to anoint the corpse.

• They experience three shocks of escalating intensity:

   – the huge stone had been "rolled away" from the tomb's entrance

   – instead of Jesus' body, they saw "a young man dressed in a white robe" in the tomb

   – the young man told them: "He has risen!"

• The Gospels alone tell us of eleven different instances when Jesus was seen after his death – at different times, in different places to different people. He ate with them, talked with them and walked with them, just as he did before his death. In 1 Corinthians 15:6 we read that five hundred people saw Jesus at one time.

• "For he [God] has set a day when he will judge the world with justice by the man he has appointed. He has given proof of this to all men by raising him [Jesus] from the dead" (Acts 17:31). The resurrection proves that Jesus will "judge the world." It also warns us that after death people will be raised to face judgement.

• The resurrection is a great hope, because it proves that there will be eternal life for those who put their trust in what Christ did at the cross. Everything that Jesus has promised will come to pass... "just as he told you."

➤ *Use the questions displayed at the end of the talk to encourage discussion. The questions are printed below and are also in the participant's* Study Guide *for reference.*

• **"Heaven is not a pipe dream, or a cruel mirage, but an amazing reality earned for us by Christ's death, and proved by Christ's resurrection." Has this changed your view of heaven?**

• **"For God has set a day when he will judge the world with justice by the man he has appointed. He has given proof of this to all men by raising him from the dead" (Acts 17:31). What's your reaction to this?**

• **Do you believe the resurrection is possible?**

yes it possible it did happen.

HOME STUDY

27th May

➤ *Read Mark 14:1 – 16:8.*

Summary: Jesus goes willingly to his death on the cross and so fulfills God's purposes.

Participants are asked to work through the following questions to help them understand the passage. They also have a section in which to write down any issues they'd like to discuss next time.

➤ *Look through the questions and answers below ahead of time so you will be able to deal with any issues that arise next week. The ADDITIONAL NOTES FOR LEADERS on page 98 will also help you to prepare.*

CHRISTIANITY
EXPLORED

1 How do we know that Jesus' death was not a mistake or accident? (see Mark 14:12–31, 48–49, 61–62)

Jesus predicted and prepared for his death. He is in total control.

Kind of detail that is there.

2 Even though Jesus knew it was his mission to die, was death easy for Jesus? (see Mark 14:33–36; 15:34)

Jesus' agony in the garden of Gethsemane and his cry of abandonment on the cross show just how hard his death was.

3 What does his death accomplish? (see Mark 15:38)

Jesus' death opens the way to God as shown by the tearing of the temple curtain from top to bottom.

Salvation. Barrier is removed curtain torn in two.

4 Although the disciples understand who Jesus is, they still haven't grasped why he has to die. What does this passage say about how people will respond if they understand who Jesus is, but not why he had to die? (see Mark 14:50, 66–71; 16:8)

Like the disciples, they will desert him.

Like Peter, they will disown him.

Like the women, they will be afraid and say nothing to anyone.

5 Who does see and understand? (see Mark 15:39) Why is that surprising?

A Roman centurion sees and understands.

It is surprising because he was directly responsible for Jesus' death. (He was also a Gentile, whom the Jews believed would not be saved.)

6 Jesus' resurrection demonstrates his power over death. What answer do you have to the inevitability of death?

This question is designed to help participants apply what they have learned.

"Feast of Unleavened Bread... Passover lamb" (Mark 14:12) – God commanded Israel to observe the annual feasts of Passover and Unleavened Bread to remind them of how he had rescued them from slavery in Egypt (Exodus 12:14–20). Israel could only be saved from the tenth plague, the plague on the firstborn, by killing a lamb, eating its roasted flesh with bitter herbs and unleavened bread, and smearing the blood on the door frames. When God saw blood on a house, he passed over it and spared the firstborn (Exodus 12:1–13). The meal eaten in Mark 14:12–26 takes place at Passover. Jesus' death would be the true means of rescue from God's judgement; it would be the true Passover. This is why Jesus is sometimes referred to as the Lamb of God.

"Blood of the covenant" (Mark 14:24) – Not only did Passover commemorate rescue from slavery in Egypt and from the wrath of God by the pouring out of blood (Exodus 12:23), but that rescue was followed by a covenant that was ratified by a blood sacrifice (Exodus 24:6). Jesus' sacrificial death mirrors this. His blood was shed on our behalf to avert God's wrath and to inaugurate a new covenant.

"Take this cup from me" (Mark 14:36) – The cup of God's wrath (Jeremiah 25:15–16).

Why do we stop reading at Mark 16:8? – Most scholars agree that Mark's Gospel ends at chapter 16:8. The women flee still partially blind, like Peter, who had himself just denied Christ three times (Mark 14:66–72). The ending provokes the question: Are you able to see who Jesus is, why he came, and what it means to follow him? (Verses 9–20 of Mark chapter 16 appear to be attempts by later writers to add a fuller resurrection ending to Mark. However, the oldest manuscripts do not include this section and its style and vocabulary are different from the rest of Mark.)

CHRISTIANITY
E✝PLORED

CHRISTIANITY EXPLORED

EXPLORING CHRISTIAN LIFE

The material in this section should be covered on a weekend or day away.

"Exploring Christian Life" aims to paint a realistic picture of what the Christian life is like and reassure people that they will not be alone if they choose to face the battles that lie ahead. Participants are given the chance to count the cost of following Christ, and they are assured that God will graciously provide the church family, his Holy Spirit, prayer and the Bible to uphold them.

It is important that people have a clear understanding of what the Christian life entails before committing to it. With that in mind, this "Exploring Christian Life" section has been placed before Weeks 7–10, when participants are invited to repent and believe.

During the weekend or day away, as in the rest of the course, there should be no corporate singing, praying or anything that could make participants feel unduly pressured or uncomfortable. Instead, leaders should seek simply to model authentic Christian living and to build sincere relationships with those in their care.

The structure of the sessions for the weekend or day away is different from the rest of the course in order to allow more time for discussion.

THE

CHURCH

TALK OUTLINE

"He who walks with the wise grows wise, but a companion of fools suffers harm." (Proverbs 13:20)

- The Christian life can be very hard, so it is important for Christians to remember that they have been chosen by God (1 Peter 1:1–2) and that they have "a living hope": the certain hope of heaven (1 Peter 1:3).

- When the Bible talks about "the church," it is simply referring to all those people who have put their trust in Jesus.

- Peter tells Christians they should "love one another deeply, from the heart" (1 Peter 1:22). Without this mutual support that the church family provides, it will be hard to persevere.

- Christians should build around them a team of wise people who will help them to follow Christ until they reach heaven.

Church is collective

Must join regularly and others.
Ensure we have company of christian
friends
Should be there for each other.

CHRISTIANITY
EXPLORED

➤ Ask participants to turn to page 46 of their Study Guide.

➤ Use the questions displayed at the end of the talk to encourage discussion. The questions are printed below and are also in the participant's Study Guide for reference.

• **"He who walks with the wise grows wise, but a companion of fools suffers harm" (Proverbs 13:20). Do you think this is true in your own experience?** *T.V. Books*

• **"...love one another deeply, from the heart" (1 Peter 1:22). Do you think this is realistic?**

EXPLORING CHRISTIAN LIFE

THE

HOLY SPIRIT

TALK OUTLINE

"It is for your good that I am going away. Unless I go away, the Counsellor will not come to you; but if I go, I will send him to you." (John 16:7)

• The Holy Spirit ("the Counsellor") who comes to live in Christians is the Spirit of Christ himself.

• The Holy Spirit's work has many aspects. For example, he:

  – makes people aware of their sin

  – changes Christians from within by giving them the desire to please God

  – gives each Christian gifts to be used in the service of other Christians

  – brings peace that comes from being in relationship with God

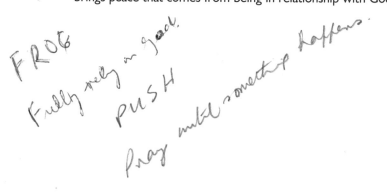

CHRISTIANITY
EXPLORED

GROUP DISCUSSION

➤ Ask participants to turn to page 47 of their Study Guide.

➤ Use the questions displayed at the end of the talk to encourage discussion. The questions are printed below and are also in the participant's Study Guide for reference.

- **"I had no inner peace." What is it that makes people feel like this?**

- **Having explored Jesus' life, how would you feel about his Spirit coming to live "with you" and "in you" (John 14:17)?**

ADDITIONAL NOTES FOR LEADERS

"another Counsellor" (John 14:16) – The word "another" in the Greek means "just the same as." So the Holy Spirit is another Counsellor, just the same as Jesus.

"Spirit of truth" (John 14:17; 15:26; 16:13; 1 John 4:6) – Jesus reassured the apostles in John 14:26 that the Holy Spirit would enable them to remember his teachings and lead them into all truth. As we read the Bible, we can be sure of its trustworthy, divine authorship.

Why does Jesus refer to the Holy Spirit as "him"? (see for example John 14:17) – The Holy Spirit – like Christ himself – is to be respected. He is not an impersonal force or an energy to be manipulated. He is the one through whom we have a relationship with the Father and the Son (John 14:23); he is not an "it."

➤ The New Testament lists the gifts of the Spirit in four passages: Romans 12:6–8; 1 Corinthians 12:8–10; Ephesians 4:11; 1 Peter 4:10–11. You may want to look at these passages with the participants if this topic is of interest to them.

EXPLORING CHRISTIAN LIFE

PRAYER

TALK OUTLINE

"Trust in him at all times, O people; pour out your hearts to him, for God is our refuge." (Psalm 62:8)   *James ch 1 V 5-8*
LUKE 11 V 5-8 .

• Christians pray in order to deepen their relationship with God.

LUKE 18 V1 - 8

• Jesus teaches his followers to address God as "Our Father." A Christian's relationship with God is a privileged, intimate one.   *LUKE 18 V 10-14*

• When Christians pray, they are praying to the "Sovereign Lord" who is in complete control of everything that may happen.   *MATT 6 V 5-6-7*

GROUP DISCUSSION

MARK 13 V 3

➤ Ask participants to turn to page 48 of their Study Guide. *M. 15 - V 8*

➤ Use the questions displayed at the end of the talk to encourage discussion. The questions are printed below and are also in the participant's Study Guide for reference.

• **Do you ever pray?**

• **God is "the Sovereign Lord, who is in complete control of everything that may happen to you." How might this affect your life?**

Amos 3 V 6

CHRISTIANITY
E✟PLORED

EXPLORING CHRISTIAN LIFE

THE

BIBLE

TALK OUTLINE

"All Scripture is God-breathed." (2 Timothy 3:16) *2 Pet. Ch 1 v 21*

- The Bible contains all kinds of writing – history, poetry, prophecy, songs, biography – but whatever the style, the message is the same: how we can be rescued from our sin. *Book*

- Reading the Bible enables Christians to know God. *Book*

- The Christian's "delight is in the law of the LORD, and on his law he meditates day and night" (Psalm 1:2). The Bible shapes the thinking of Christian people.

- "He is like a tree planted by streams of water" (Psalm 1:3). The Christian is refreshed and replenished by reading the Bible. *over*

- "Mary has chosen what is better" (Luke 10:42). Christians must choose to make time to read God's word, no matter how busy their lives become. *over* *Book .*

➤ Ask participants to turn to page 49 of their Study Guide.

➤ Use the questions displayed at the end of the talk to encourage discussion. The questions are printed below and are also in the participant's Study Guide for reference.

• **"Mary has chosen what is better" (Luke 10:42). What choices do you need to make to hear God's word?**

Be where I can hear it. Make time for reading the Bible

• **The person who delights in God's word is "like a tree planted by streams of water, which yields its fruit in season" (Psalm 1:3). Do you think the Bible could play this role in your life?**

The more you study the more you manage to absorb. you get stale & dry if you do not keep refreshing yourself with the Bible.

➤ Be ready to offer practical advice to participants on how they can begin reading the Bible regularly. It may be useful to have Bible reading notes available to help participants who want to do this. You may also want to share with participants how and when you do your own personal study of the Bible.

Do my crossword with my breakfast cuppa. Not up or only a music grates in the way of that. I decided to do my daily readings then. Night time I'm too tired. Too busy & hurried later in day. Find a good time

WHAT IS

A CHRISTIAN?

GROUP DISCUSSION 1

AND PETER V 7 cl 16

➤ Ask participants to turn to Week 7 on page 51 of their Study Guide.

➤ Ask if anyone has any questions arising from last week's HOME STUDY, and discuss as necessary. *Who is young man in V 51 ch 14.*

V 32 cl 15 THOSE CRUCIFIED WITH HIM HEAPED INSULTS ON HIM

➤ Ask participants to turn to Mark 14:1–11. One of the leaders should read the passage aloud and then the group should work through the study below. The answers are printed here for your reference. The ADDITIONAL NOTES FOR LEADERS on page 108 may also help you.

1 How do the different people in this passage respond to Jesus?	
HUMAN → DIVINE	
Jesus had 2 faces	**RESPONSE TO JESUS**
The religious leaders *V 1*	They plot to arrest and kill Jesus.
"Some of those present" *John 12 V 4 & 6*	They are indignant at what the woman does for Jesus. They see it as wasteful. *Matt 26 V 8*
The woman *V 3*	She "does what she can" – she acts out of generosity and love.
Judas *V 10*	He plots to betray Jesus and looks for an opportunity to hand Jesus over to the religious leaders. He agrees to take money for this betrayal.

2 How does Jesus respond to what the woman does for him? Why? (see Mark 14:6–8)

He sees it as a "beautiful thing" to do for him. He accepts her anointing as preparation for his burial because he knows his death is imminent.

3 Would Jesus have been surprised at the plotting of the religious leaders?

No, he'd already predicted what would happen (see Mark 8:31).

4 Would Jesus have been surprised at Judas' scheme?

No, he knows what Judas is doing (see Mark 14:18).

5 What does Mark 14:9 tell us about Jesus?

He knows everything that will happen. The fact that we're discussing this incident now proves Jesus right: 2000 years later, no matter where in the world we are, this woman's actions are still being retold.

6 So how should we respond to Jesus?

This question is designed to help participants apply what they have learned.

ADDITIONAL NOTES FOR LEADERS

Perfume (Mark 14:3) – It was the custom to pour a few drops of perfume on a guest when he arrived at a house or sat down to a meal. This woman, however, broke open an entire jar. It was also the custom to anoint the bodies of the dead with perfume.

"The poor you will always have with you" (Mark 14:7) – Jesus quotes Deuteronomy 15:11.

"If anyone would come after me, he must deny himself and take up his cross and follow me." (Mark 8:34)

- In Mark chapter 8, we see that Jesus' disciples have begun to recognize who he is. Peter identifies Jesus as "the Christ," that is, the King promised in the Old Testament who would have the power and authority of God himself.

- Jesus then teaches them that he came to die. He knows that the only way sinful people can be brought back into a relationship with God is by dying in their place.

- Then Jesus says, "If anyone would come after me, he must deny himself and take up his cross and follow me."

    – Denying self means no longer living for ourselves but for Jesus.

    – Taking up our cross means being prepared to follow him, whatever the cost.

- Jesus gives a convincing reason to live like this: "What good is it for a man to gain the whole world, yet forfeit his soul?" (Mark 8:36).

GROUP DISCUSSION 2

➤ *Use the questions displayed at the end of the talk to encourage discussion. The questions are printed below and are also in the participant's* Study Guide *for reference.*

man in video was partially said

- **"What good is it for a man to gain the whole world, yet forfeit his soul?" (Mark 8:36). How would *you* answer that question?**

- **Jesus said: "If anyone would come after me, he must deny himself and take up his cross and follow me" (Mark 8:34). Do you feel you could do this?**

- **"A Christian is someone who is prepared to follow Christ, whatever the cost." What is the cost?** *Sometimes you lose friends or family. Choose to live differently*

WEEK 7

➤ *Participants have been asked to read Ephesians 2:1–22. Read the passage and look in advance at the study on pages 111–112 to help you prepare to lead participants through the study next week.*

Note: The participant's Study Guide *contains the following "prayer of commitment." The course leader will read it aloud at the end of this week and again at the end of Week 10. You may want to refer to it yourself if a participant tells you they want to begin following Christ at any point during the course.*

If you've become convinced of who Jesus is and what he came to do, and you understand what it will mean to follow him, you might like to pray the following prayer:

Heavenly Father, I have rebelled against you. I have sinned in my thoughts, my words and my actions – sometimes unconsciously, sometimes deliberately. I am sorry for the way I have lived and ask you to forgive me. Thank you that Jesus died on the cross so that I could be forgiven. Thank you that I can now see clearly who Jesus is and why he came. Please send your Holy Spirit to help me follow him whatever the cost. Amen.

CHRISTIANITY
E✝PLORED

CONTINUING

AS A CHRISTIAN

GROUP DISCUSSION 1

➤ Ask participants to turn to Week 8 on page 55 of their Study Guide.

➤ Ask participants to turn to Ephesians 2:1–10. One of the leaders should read the passage aloud and then the group should work through the study below. The answers are printed here for your reference.

---

1 How does Paul describe human beings in Ephesians 2:1–3?

Dead in transgressions and sins (v. 1).

Following the ways of the world and the devil (v. 2).

Disobedient (v. 2).

Gratifying the desires of their sinful nature (v. 3).

Objects of God's wrath (v. 3).

2 How is the Christian described in Ephesians 2:4–10?

Alive with Christ (v. 5).

Saved (v. 5).

Raised up with Christ and seated with him in the heavenly realms (v. 6).

Doing good works (v. 10).

---

3 What is it that makes the difference between the person described in verses 1–3 and the person described in verses 4–10? (see Ephesians 2:4–5)

God's grace: he saves people in his great love and mercy.

4 In what way does salvation come to us from God? (see Ephesians 2:8)

Through faith. It is a gift that we receive.

5 What is the appropriate response to God's grace? (see Ephesians 2:9–10)

Not to boast because it is all God's work (v. 9); to do good works (v. 10).

6 What can you contribute to your salvation?

Nothing. Even faith itself is a gift from God. (There may be those who have always thought that you trust in good works in order to be accepted by God. They believe they are accepted by being good enough, giving to charity, not lying, being a good citizen, going to church, praying, being baptized, or whatever. The passage makes it clear this is not the case.)

CHRISTIANITY
E≯PLORED

"Jesus said, 'It is finished.'" (John 19:30)

- Christians will face opposition: from the world around them, from their own sinful nature, and also from the devil, who wants to undermine the Christian's relationship with God.

- There are certain things Christians can be sure of in the face of opposition:

    - the presence of the Holy Spirit, who gives Christians the desire and the strength to overcome this opposition.

    - the promises of God in the Bible that provide assurance of God's love and sovereign power.

    - Christ died to pay for sin past, present and future. "There is now no condemnation for those who are in Christ Jesus" (Romans 8:1).

- As he died, Jesus said, "It is finished." No matter how hard life gets, these words remind Christians that their sin is paid for, they're at peace with God and destined to be with him in heaven.

➤ *Use the questions displayed at the end of the talk to encourage discussion. The questions are printed below and are also in the participant's* Study Guide *for reference.*

• **Do you feel able to trust God's promises in the Bible?**

• **Can you see how Jesus' words – "It is finished" (John 19:30) – might affect your life?**

Past Present ~ Future.

HOME STUDY

➤ *Participants have been asked to re-read Mark 3:1 – 4:41. Read the passage and look in advance at the study on pages 115–116 to help you prepare to lead participants through the study next week.*

CHRISTIANITY
E✝PLORED

CHOICES

- KING HEROD

GROUP DISCUSSION 1

➤ Ask participants to turn to Week 9 on page 59 of their Study Guide.

➤ Ask participants to turn to Mark 4:3–20. One of the leaders should read the passage aloud and then the group should work through the study below. The answers are printed here for your reference. The ADDITIONAL NOTES FOR LEADERS on page 116 may also help you.

---

1 After telling the parable in verses 3–8, Jesus interprets it in verses 13–20. So, what does the "seed" represent?

The word of God.

2 What are the four possible outcomes when God's word is preached? (see Mark 4:15–20)

v. 15   Satan comes and takes the word away.

vv. 16–17   The word is received with joy but it has no root, so when trouble or persecution comes the hearer gives up.

vv. 18–19   The "worries of this life, the deceitfulness of wealth and the desires for other things" choke the word.

v. 20   The word is heard, accepted and produces a lasting effect.

WEEK 9

3 What does it mean if the hearer has "no root"? (see Mark 4:17)

Their response never goes beneath the surface; it remains shallow and superficial. As a result, peer pressure or opposition will cause them to give up.

4 How do the "worries of this life, the deceitfulness of wealth and the desires for other things" choke the word?

These things are in direct conflict with God's word and, if we allow them to determine our choices, we will face dire consequences. If our time, energy and resources are focused on these things, they cannot be focused on God. There is a choice to be made – as Jesus said, "No-one can serve two masters" (Matthew 6:24).

5 How have *you* responded to hearing God's word?

This question is designed to reveal where the participants stand with Christ.

ADDITIONAL NOTES FOR LEADERS

Parable of the sower (Mark 4:3–20) – Throughout Mark chapter 3, opposition to Jesus has been growing. Jesus responds in Mark chapter 4 by teaching about the power of the word.

CHRISTIANITY
EXPLORED

"The king was greatly distressed, but because of his oaths and his dinner guests, he did not want to refuse her." (Mark 6:26)

• King Herod was deliberately rebelling against God.

• John the Baptist, a man Herod knew was "righteous and holy," repeatedly warned him to stop rebelling. But Herod would not turn away from what he knew was wrong – he would not repent.

• Finally, on Herod's birthday, "the opportune time came." His wife asked for John the Baptist's head on a platter. Herod had a choice: he could either repent, or give her what she wanted. Under pressure from his wife, his friends and his dinner guests, Herod once again chose not to repent.

• Later in life, Herod meets Jesus. "He plied him with many questions, but Jesus gave him no answer" (Luke 23:9). Rejecting Jesus' call to repent and believe may earn us the approval of other people, but it will eventually earn us the rejection of Jesus.

WEEK 9

➤ Use the questions displayed at the end of the talk to encourage discussion. The questions are printed below and are also in the participant's Study Guide for reference.

- **Why do you think Herod refused to repent?**

- **John's preaching greatly disturbed Herod. How does Jesus' teaching make you feel?**

HOME STUDY

➤ Participants have been asked to note down any questions they still have.

CHRISTIANITY
E✝PLORED

TRIFLE. ✓ CREAM.

CHOICES - JAMES, JOHN & BARTIMAEUS

GROUP DISCUSSION 1

➤ Ask participants to turn to Week 10 on page 63 of their Study Guide.

➤ Use the time to discuss any questions participants may have.

TALK OUTLINE

"'What do you want me to do for you?' Jesus asked." (Mark 10:36 and 51)

• James and John ask Jesus for power and prestige. So Jesus knows that they cannot have understood what it means to follow him. He corrects their thinking by reminding them that even he "did not come to be served, but to serve, and to give his life as a ransom for many" (Mark 10:45).

• If you've already put your trust in Jesus, you may need to learn what James and John learned: following Jesus is about service, not status.

• Bartimaeus asks for mercy. Jesus heals him. He immediately begins to follow Jesus.

• If you haven't yet put your trust in Jesus, you need to do what Bartimaeus did: cry out to him for mercy and follow him.

➤ Use the questions displayed at the end of the talk to encourage discussion. The questions are printed below and are also in the participant's Study Guide for reference.

• **Who do you identify with most: James and John or Bartimaeus?**

• **What choices will you make based on what you've learned during Christianity Explored?**

➤ In Week 1, participants were asked for their answer to the following question: "If you could ask God one question, and you knew it would be answered, what would it be?" Ask participants to repeat the exercise now and compare their answer with the answer they gave in Week 1.

Note: The participant's Study Guide contains the following "prayer of commitment." The course leader will read it aloud at the end of this week. You may want to refer to it yourself if a participant tells you they want to begin following Christ at any point after the course.

Thank you for making time to attend **Christianity Explored**. If you've become convinced of who Jesus is and what he came to do, and you understand what it will mean to follow him, you might like to pray the following prayer:

Heavenly Father, I have rebelled against you. I have sinned in my thoughts, my words and my actions – sometimes unconsciously, sometimes deliberately. I am sorry for the way I have lived and ask you to forgive me. Thank you that Jesus died on the cross so that I could be forgiven. Thank you that I can now see clearly who Jesus is and why he came. Please send your Holy Spirit to help me follow him whatever the cost. Amen.

Notes

Week 7 Mark / Kath.

" 8 Jonathan / Hugh

" 9 Ronald / Agnes

10 Mark Kath.

Table 1
Ronald Mark Hugh.

Table 2

Kath
Agnes
Jonathan.

Notes

Jesus gave man partial sight
just.

Then sight restored.

We are like that. It is

gradual sometimes.

What do we see

Do we see only human
face
or can we see divine face
too.

Eyes are only half open.
They need to be opened fully
when Jesus teaches them
more about himself they
begin to see
He came to die
It's necessary to die
Only many sinful people

can be brought back.
Why did he have to die?
When he told the story of
the man in the water we did
not have the whole story
we need the whole story
The man gave his life to
save others.
Similarly we need to know the
whole story about Jesus before
we can make up our minds.
This course helps us to find
out the whole story. Read
the Bible.
2 things. deny ourselves
Take up our cross.
Notice Take up our cross
he take it willingly. Its not
something we have to bear. Its
chosen. I will die for you but
you must be prepared to take up
your cross too

Notes

2 we will face suffering.
Misunderstood. Family may not
like the change in us. Opposition.
Christians is prepared to follow
Jesus whatever the cost.

Too light a price?

3 Our souls are the most precious
things we have. Choose whether
the judge is our Saviour.
Jesus will treat us in
the same way as we have
treated him. Sober thoughts
gold jewels, priceless treasure
of no us in Eternity.

Notes

Notes

Notes

Notes